Exceptional Plants

'Stephen Ryan has an enviable facility for conveying the look and personality of a plant so that it springs before the inward eye. His writing is not only informative, but friendly and light-hearted, so that the reader feels it would be a pleasure to meet him as well as the plants he describes.'

Christopher Lloyd, Great Dixter, East Sussex, UK

Exceptional Plants

100 Trees and Shrubs to Give Your Garden the Edge

Stephen Ryan

HYLAND  HOUSE

First published in Australia in 1999 by
Hyland House Publishing Pty Ltd
Hyland House
387-389 Clarendon Street
South Melbourne
Victora 3205

National Library of Australia
Cataloguing-in-publication data

Ryan, Stephen Godfrey.
Exceptional plants: 100 trees and shrubs to give your garden the edge.

Includes index.
ISBN 1 86447 075 5.

1. Trees – Australia Encyclopedias. 2. Shrubs – Australia Encyclopedias. I. Title. II. Title: One hundred trees and shrubs to give your garden the edge.

582.1603

Editing by Vida Horn
Cover design by Jo Waite
Typeset in-house by Hyland House
Produced by Phoenix Offset Hong Kong

Contents

Contents

Contents

Botanical Names

Botanical names and their origins have been verified as far as possible, using the frequently conflicting authorieties listed in the bibliography on page 206. Unfortunately the most recent publication does not necessarily have the most recently established name.

Measurements

The ultimate maximum size of any plant will depend on a number of factors, including soil, span of hours of sunlight, orientation, atmospheric humidity, water and nutrients. The sizes given in this book are for trees and shrubs grown under average to good conditions and will obviously vary for each plant; so will the size of leaves and flowers.

Both metric and roughly approximate imperial measurements are given.

Introduction

I have always been a plant collector. Not for me though the restraints of a single genus. The men and women who collect every known dahlia or old-fashioned rose with single-minded devotion are worthy persons indeed; we need them and their collections for all the reasons you can probably list yourself.

For me it is the fun of the plant kingdom as a whole that attracts so I flit from one acquisition to the next, enjoying the hunt and the final capture of something on my wish list, or meeting a complete unknown that suddenly turns up.

I get even more than most out of this pursuit as I making my living out of my passion. Since 1980 I have run my own nursery, Dicksonia Rare Plants, at Mount Macedon in Victoria, Australia.

With its good gardening climate (cool to cold moist winters with light frost, warm usually dry summers and deep dark humus-rich soil), I couldn't be in a better spot. At least you would think so, but like all keen gardeners I would love to grow what I shouldn't. Rhododendrons and maples flourish here, but why can't I have bougainvilleas and frangipani? When I have the money I will build an enormous heated glasshouse and have the best of both worlds.

In the meantime, I like to read about all kinds of plants, as gardeners do all over the world. This book is meant for the eager gardener who would like to know more about exceptionally good trees and shrubs. I hope it will also appeal to the armchair horticulturist who reads about plants and gardens for enjoyment as well as for information. As you can see, it is not a giant A to Z reference tome, nor is it a garden do-it-yourself practical manual. It is intended to be a fun read full of interesting trees and shrubs, one hundred in all, incorporating as I go along some of my gardening philosophies. Most of the profiles have something about the origin of the botanical and common name (where there is one) and the history of the introduction of that particular plant. This gives it extra individuality, and can be a guide to growing conditions.

It all started when I was approached by Tim and Keva North to write plant profiles for their magazine *The Australian Garden Journal*. This I did religiously, if not always on time, until the Norths decided to give up publishing the *Journal*, and sadly it is no more.

Then I was approached by Anne and Al at Hyland House to write a book. As I had never written a book before I was highly flattered. I suggested my previously printed plant profiles as a lazy way for me to get into hardback.

It was pointed out that it would be a very slim volume and I would have to write at least another sixty profiles. The results I would now like to put before you.

Finally, I must acknowledge the help and support I have had in getting this far:

My parents for having me as well as having faith in me.

Craig, my partner, for pushing and bullying me into finishing the manuscript.

The Royal Horticultural Society of Victoria for publishing me first, in their now long-gone magazine *Gardening News*.

Tim and Keva North for the inspiration to write the original plant profiles.

Everyone at Hyland House, especially Anne Godden, who kindly looked after me and didn't push me as she should have when my work wasn't done.

And finally, Vida Horn, whose classical Latin and eye for detail have kept me and my writings on the straight and narrow.

Stephen Ryan, 1999

Abelia floribunda

'*Is it bushy?*' I often get slightly tired of this question, usually asked about shrubs. People seem to want a garden full of vegetable plum puddings. I know that there are many aspects within our gardens that require something with a bushy habit. After all, we often need something dense enough to hide the clothes line or to screen our strange behaviour from prying neighbours. But there are many lax-growing shrubs that can be most appealing in our landscape and that aren't being grown simply because they don't have this supposedly valuable character.

An arching elegant form isn't just a nurseryman's euphemism for straggly, although this can be hard to justify when presenting a customer with a gawky young pot-grown specimen. Plants of a lax, arching habit can have many uses in the garden. They can lighten up an otherwise stodgy planting, be allowed to spill over or through other plants, trained as espalier plants against walls, or even grown as weeping standards.

A plant that could fit the bill for all of the above is *Abelia floribunda*, from Mexico. It is the most spectacular species of its genus, which I don't think is saying all that much. Abelias are, as a group, rather ordinary, with small foliage and little trumpet-shaped flowers, usually in shades of white and mauve. Most are rather leggy shrubs and in gardens they end up being trimmed, making them all the more ungainly, instead of being thinned out, which if you have to have them would be a better technique.

A. floribunda has a very arching habit that no amount of trimming is going to change, so it can look very straggly in a 20 cm (8 in) pot, but once installed in the garden will make a lovely open mound that will take advantage of any purchase offered by neighbouring shrubs. Freestanding plants will rarely exceed 2 metres (6 ft) in height, but can often grow much wider. If you decide to train it as a wall shrub, either on its own or in combination with other plants, it can be encouraged to quite a height and specimens up to 7 metres (23 ft) have been recorded.

Because of its rather open habit it won't swamp anything growing with or near it, and its glossy green leaves and reddish twigs will look pleasant all year round. It is, however, whilst in bloom that it will really show its stuff. The flowers are the biggest in the genus, about 5 cm long by 2.5 cm wide (2 in by 1 in), are a rich cherry-pink in colour with white inside the trumpets and are produced in large quantities during the summer months.

This species is hardy in Australia and New Zealand, requiring nothing more than an open sunny aspect and well-drained soil. The rest is up to you. They are easily propagated from cuttings, in fact I often find self-layered plants around my specimen, and will grow quite quickly to fill any allotted space in the garden.

Pruning, when necessary, should be done straight after flowering, so as not to remove any of the current season's blooms, but tying in or training should be an ongoing chore as its long and wayward branches can be quite brittle and easily broken.

The genus consists of some fifteen species with a rather disjointed distribution. Most are native to China, Japan and the Himalayas with a few, including our subject, native to the mountains of Mexico. They belong to the Honeysuckle family, Caprifoliaceae.

The abelia was named after Dr Clarke Abel (1780-1826), who discovered the first species, *A. chinensis*, whilst he was physician to Lord Amherst's embassy to China in 1816-1817. Like many others he wrote a book about his adventures, called rather unimaginatively *Narrative of a Journey in the Interior of China*.

Due to him *Abelia* is often first cab off the rank in alphabetical listings of shrubs in garden books, a position that it wouldn't deserve on merit. However even if you don't grow any other species in this genus, you should definitely find room for *Abelia floribunda*.

Abeliophyllum distichum

Sometimes a plant languishes in obscurity for no apparent reason. If you analyse the reasons it is often due to nothing more than the fact that as the plant isn't known to start with obviously no-one asks for it, so the nursery trade doesn't grow or supply it. This is of course a vicious circle and unless someone (like me) starts to promote the qualities of the said plant it will always have a limited audience. It is a case of nurseries being more trend followers than trend setters.

You can't really blame the trade too much for this attitude. They have to make a living and as things like azaleas will sell themselves (worst luck) whereas some unknown beauty with a name like *Bloomingthingia roadsidia* will have to be persuasively sold, can you blame these poor people who probably have children to feed?

This is all leading to an obscure beauty called *Abeliophyllum distichum*, which has the added drawback of flowering in late winter.

You may wonder why I say that flowering as it does in a period of the year when flowers can be scarce is a drawback at all, it should be a positive bonus. But when it is flowering the weather can be bleak, which discourages nursery visitors, so that a minimum see it in flower.

I am the first to admit that it isn't a shrub that inspires awe when not in bloom so it often takes some talking to convince prospective purchasers to try it.

During the summer months it has mid green foliage similar in shape to that of an abelia, as the generic name suggests. This is hardly a recommendation that will move stock.

Although it becomes an attractive arching shape with age, as a young plant it could be described as straggly, another point against it.

In the autumn its foliage will turn pale yellow before shedding, again nothing exciting but we are slowly getting to the point of it all.

In winter until it blooms my customers could easily be forgiven for thinking that I was selling dead stock. Its twigs are brown and its dormant flower buds are almost black. It really shows no evidence of life to the uninitiated.

All will be forgiven in late winter, however, when the black buds erupt with lovely white forsythia-like blooms that are pink-stained in bud and wonderfully fragrant when fully open. Now you might think you have obtained a semi-dwarf, arching, scented white forsythia and they are in fact related, both belonging to the Olive family, Oleaceae.

It could be trained up a wall or fence to 2 metres (6ft) tall but as a freestanding shrub usually grows little more than half this height. The arching canes will obligingly fill any odd-shaped gap you wish to allow for it.

The only regular care it should have is to completely remove some of the older spent canes that have become unproductive, although I usually prune them out whilst they are still putting in some effort when in full bloom. This way, I can have my flowers and prune it too.

Sprays of flowers could be used in the house, where its scent will be more comfortably appreciated at a time when flowers can be a little scarce.

Abeliophyllum seems to be quite hardy as long as the weather doesn't become too hot and dry. It isn't fussy about soil types although the better the soil is the better it will do, quite obviously!

New plants can be propagated from summer cuttings or if you aren't good at this you could easily layer some tips down.

This attractive small shrub will be useful planted in a border amongst later flowered

subjects to extend the season and you could always underplant it with *Galanthus nivalis*, the snowdrop, for a charming white-on-white effect.

Its native habitat is the mountains of Korea. It was introduced into cultivation in 1924, so horticulturally speaking it could be said to be quite new. It gained an Award of Merit in 1937 and a First Class Certificate in 1944, so someone must have appreciated it.

Finally, Richmond E. Harrison in his *Handbook of Trees and Shrubs* suggests that 'it should find a place in good gardens'. If you have a bad garden perhaps this isn't for you.

Acer pentaphyllum

I regularly have customers who for some reason have decided to make a Japanese garden. If my nursery were in Japan, it would seem quite natural. However in a hot dry Australian summer the concept of Japanese maples underplanted with spongy moss is quite impractical.

Of course I am not immune to the charm of Japanese landscaping, just as I can see beauty in the Mogul gardens of India or in virtually any style of gardening, but I think that a slavishly reproduced copy in an alien setting can look quite grotesque.

What we should all aim to do is find the spirit of the style and adapt it to our own needs. The way in which the Japanese use rock and water has much to teach the rest of us, as does the way they place and prune plant material.

Selecting plants that exhibit the right feel is often all it takes to set the right mood. When we see a cactus, we can quite easily visualise the desert. This doesn't mean that if we wish to get an oriental feel we have to use bamboo, although it certainly helps. I find some Australian native plants have a distinctly oriental flavour and may well make good alternatives. It is, however, about a plant that not only looks oriental, but is in fact a native of China, that I wish to write.

Acer pentaphyllum is probably the world's rarest maple, with reputedly some two or three hundred trees in the wild along the Yalong River in Szechuan, and must be regarded a real newcomer to the western world. It was discovered in 1929 by Joseph Rock (1884-1962) and, depending on which reference you use, he either collected it then and there or introduced it much later after another working holiday in China. The first trees were raised at the Strybing Arboretum in San Francisco and all now growing in Western horticulture are supposed to have originated from them.

For purposes of botanical description the large and varied *Acer* genus is divided into sections. *A. pentaphyllum*, which is a quite unique and different-looking maple, is the only species in the Pentaphylla section. It will, however, graft quite well onto some of the larger-leafed species like *A. pseudoplatanus*, the sycamore. This is just as well, because it seems at least in Europe and America not to set seed, although I do know it has done so for at least one Australian grower. I would generally recommend a grafted specimen as the rootstock tends to make a much more vigorous tree.

Although it is not considered to be fully hardy to the cold in England, I have found it to be suprisingly tolerant of heat and wind for a maple and I would like to recommend using it more.

It makes a nice slightly spreading small tree to about 10 metres (30 ft) with pleasant fibrous bone-coloured bark and very dainty-looking leaves divided into five slender leaflets. Its foliage does in fact have a bamboo-like quality, obviously why it has a distinctly oriental look. Because of the fine nature of the leaves the shade it casts is not heavy, so it would make an ideal tree under which many other plants will flourish.

In mid to late autumn it will turn lovely shades of yellow and orange. Although the autumn shades aren't a match for many of the Japanese maple cultivars it usually happens quite a bit later, so by the time it turns it usually has little competition. A subtle and charming end to the season.

Although its summer foliage is a nice but unremarkable shade of green, it has great presence due partly to its shape and to the fact that its petioles are red. Petioles for those that

are wondering are the leaf stems: the bit that sheds with the leaf in autumn and holds it on the branch for the rest of the time. Although coloured petioles don't have the impact of flowers, they often add greatly to the value of the plant.

Lastly, I should mention that *A. pentaphyllum* is a very late starter in spring and for many people this could be seen as a major drawback. But for late winter and early spring flowering bulbs like snowdrops and crocus, it allows longer for their leaves to feed the bulb before the canopy returns.

In districts where it performs well, I might suggest that a copse of *Acer pentaphyllum* could be a lot more up-market and less predictable than the ever-present silver birch and maybe an even better choice under which to establish a bluebell wood.

Anopterus glandulosus

It always amazes me that in this country we have the decision 'Will we go native or won't we?'

In most countries the question most gardeners ask is 'Will this plant do the job required of it?' not 'Where does it come from?'

After all, what are those national borders we inflict on plants? If history had been a little different, Western Australia might well have been settled by someone other than the British and thus become a separate country. Had New Zealand joined us at Federation their flora would then have been Australian. New Guinea was ours for some time and the Australian National Botanic Gardens in Canberra had Vireya rhododendrons from New Guinea on display (they may still have).

Tasmania, as we all know, is an island with a remarkable flora that includes many endemic species. Just as easily it too could have been a separate country (some people seem to think it still is!).

This leads me to one of my favourite Tasmanian native plants, one that most native plant growers don't seem to stock and one which some of them may not even know about.

The plant is question is *Anopterus glandulosus*, or Tasmanian Native Laurel. When you first see it in flower you could be excused for believing that it is ericaceous. It does have leathery rich green foliage clustered towards the top of the stems, rather like a rhododendron, and the lovely flowers remind me of kalmias and pieris. It does best in acid, moist but not wet soil with a cool aspect and looks better mixed with the plants just mentioned rather than with, say, a batch of grevilleas.

Anopterus is in fact a member of the Escallonia family (Escalloniaceae or, in some books, Saxifragaceae). It is a slow-growing shrub that may reach 2 to 3 metres (6 to 10 ft) in gardens, although it may be taller in the wild. It produces its lovely, usually white, flowers in spring. Each bell is about 1 cm (1/2 in) in diameter, and the flowers are produced in racemes up to 15 cm (6 in) long.

In beds already planted with azaleas and rhododendrons this plant will look quite at home, alternatively you may like to grow it as a tub specimen in a fernery or under trees.

The form in the photograph is the pale pink one often found in the wild but to my knowledge never given a varietal name. It is possibly an even better plant than the white form, as its leaves are darker with red petioles and dormant buds.

Arbutus glandulosa

No matter how often I visit the Royal Botanic Gardens in Melbourne there is one plant I always make a trunk call to.

It may well amaze you to think that any one plant in this huge collection could demand my presence on every visit. I love looking at all the rare, interesting and often bizarre specimens in this living museum, but at every visit I am drawn toward the kiosk. Not to get a drink or visit the Friends' Shop (although I do tend to do that as well), but to look at one particular tree nearby.

In the Beautiful Bark stakes surely *Arbutus glandulosa* must be up there with the best of them.

It is a native of southern Mexico and some botanists have suggested that it may be a minor variant of *A. xalapensis*, which I haven't seen. Apparently *A. glandulosa* has glandular hairs on its petioles and the other doesn't. Obviously not enough difference to worry us gardeners.

It would appear to be a remarkably hardy tree for Australian conditions. It is a true mystery that it hasn't become widely grown. Because it is fairly drought-tolerant and cold-hardy as well as being indifferent to acid or limey soils, it should grow well in many areas. It should also be ideal in smaller gardens as this charming evergreen grows into a small tree of only about 7.5 metres (23 ft).

I would grow it for its bark alone but it is truly attractive in all ways. The soft pink to white flowers, rather like lily-of-the-valley, are produced in late spring and summer. They are followed by large orange fruit, which are edible but unexciting. The foliage, as I have already mentioned, is evergreen; it is also large and glossy and never produced in such abundance that it casts heavy shade.

The stunning bark peels off each year during late spring and summer. It changes colour as it ages, starting greenish-white turning fawn-pink and by winter it is usually rich burnished copper.

My picture shows the tree in late spring with both its old and new bark. Also to be seen in the shot are its lovely leaves.

Its growth rate seem to be quite rapid as my own specimen is now about 2.5 metres (7 to 8 ft) tall after about five years in the ground, with a trunk about 4 cm (2 in) in diameter.

So, in conclusion, if this lovely thing has any vices I have yet to discover them; the only trouble you are likely to have is getting one.

Argyrocytisus battandieri

My title for this profile isn't quite accurate as the plant I will describe isn't really new, but it certainly has a new name. It is, however, a broom, and I felt a little poetic licence was justifiable so I didn't waste what I think is a good heading!

The plant in question is the lovely *Argyrocytisus battandieri*, which until the release of *The New Royal Horticultural Society Dictionary of Gardening* was universally known (and is still generally listed) as *Cytisus battandieri*. It can, of course, still be called by its well-accepted common name, Moroccan Broom.

The changing of plant names is, I know, a pain but in this case I feel it is probably quite fair considering how different this plant looks from the rest of the *Cytisus* genus. Although the new generic name is longer and more difficult to say (which seems to be the way these things go) it nonetheless makes sense as *argyros* is Greek for 'silver' and its relationship to its old genus is kept as well. However, it now becomes a monotypic genus, which means it consists of only one species.

Moroccan broom was introduced into cultivation from its native haunts in the Rif and Atlas Mountains in about 1922, which does make it a comparative newcomer. It received an Award of Merit in 1931, a First Class Certificate in 1934 and an Award of Garden Merit in 1984. Obviously with all these accolades it is a plant none of us should be without.

Now I had best tell you about its charms so that you will appreciate how indispensable it is.

It is a large semi-deciduous shrub to about 4 metres (13 ft), with handsome silky silver leaves rather similar in shape (but much prettier in colour) to laburnum. In summer it produces its tight clusters of rich yellow pea flowers that have a mouth-watering scent generally described as like that of pineapples. I am not so sure about the smell being pineapple, I think it much more like that of a green apple. Whatever you decide, you will have to agree that it is a deliciously fruity smell.

In England it is usually trained against a wall to protect it from extreme cold. It could certainly be grown that way here if you would like to, but it is quite happy as an open-growing freestanding plant in any sunny border.

It isn't fussy about the soil it grows in as long as it is well drained, and like other brooms it can tend to grow a bit leggy and scruffy with age. However, unlike its relatives it can be cut down to the socks and will shoot away and become a young vigorous plant again. This is an altogether desirable plant, well suited to Australian conditions, that doesn't deserve to be left in relative obscurity.

Azara integrifolia 'Variegata'

Variegated plants definitely polarise the gardening community. At one extreme you have the devotees who love coloured leaves with splashes, blotches or edges of silver and gold. They have even started societies to collect and encourage the use of variegates. At the other extreme are the detractors who can't abide all that freakish foliage that looks diseased and, as they don't hesitate to point out, is usually due to a virus anyway. These nasty viruses not only kill useful green pigments in the leaves, they also make that plant weaker of growth and less hardy to extremes than the natural green forms. Another argument used by the dissenters is that variegated leaves are vulgar and suburban and that gardeners who use them for a splash of colour are the same down-market types that use purple plastic pots for their petunias or insist on garden gnomes in football uniforms. This is, of course, completely subjective and I for one believe that these plants aren't usually inherently bad, it is more a matter of how they are used.

In other words I am one of that rarer breed of gardener who takes the middle ground on this issue, though I admit that there are some variegates that should never have seen the light of day.

I know it's very tempting for gardeners to grow any new mutation, but I certainly wouldn't wish to have a plant named after me that looked like it had leprosy. On the other hand, gardening would be the poorer without these often bold and showy plants.

All this is of course leading us to one particular variegated plant that I hope you will agree has a place in horticulture if not in your garden. If you don't like it or plant it, then I hope it will be all the more novel and interesting when you see it in my garden. The plant in question is *Azara integrifolia* 'Variegata', and I must say there isn't such a thing as a poor azara, all being very worthy evergreen shrubs and small trees.

This particular one is an elegant arching shrub usually no more than 3 metres (10 ft) tall by 2 metres (6 ft) across and it would definitely be quite an age to reach these dimensions. Its small deep green leaves are boldly edged in rich gold and they usually have some burgundy markings in the variegation. Their deep colours become even more prevalent during the colder months and are obviously not a variegation, but a beautiful cold-induced blemish.

Azaras aren't completely hardy in England, so there they are usually grown against a sheltered wall and trained up it. This isn't necessary in antipodean gardens with our milder winters, but as they look so good grown this way, why not do it anyway? The other advantage to espaliering them is that their perfume can be encouraged indoors just by opening a window.

All species in this genus have small flowers that consist of nothing more than a cluster of stamens and I must admit their mustard-yellow colour is all but lost due to the leaf colour of *A. integrifolia* 'Variegata'. They are produced on our selection in late autumn and into early winter and on any sunny day the perfume is quite strong. It is fun watching the uninitiated looking for the source and I've often been caught by my plant when I forget its blooming time. When it finishes its floral bit, it often produces pea-sized lilac-white berries, interesting at close quarters but again overpowered by its leaves.

The genetic name commemorates J.N. Azara, who was a Spanish scientist born in Aragon in 1731 and dying in Paris in 1804, and the genus consists of some ten species restricted to South America, mainly in Chile

and Argentina.

If you are still unimpressed with variegated plants, then might I suggest that you could plant some of the other species, such as *A. microphylla* or *A. serrata*. *A. microphylla* makes a small upright tree with very dark and tiny green leaves arranged on elegant fan-shaped branches. Its practically invisible flowers are produced in spring and are usually described as having a vanilla fragrance. I think it is more like the mouth-watering smell of freshly baked chocolate cake packed with calories.

Far showier in bloom is *Azara serrata*, with its golden yellow stamens somewhat reminiscent of acacia (wattle). It is only slightly scented but still makes a nice small tree with an upright and fanned habit. The leaves are larger and a lighter glossy green, making it pleasant all year.

Berberis thunbergii 'Helmond Pillar'

It is often difficult to find bold and sculptural small shrubs that would be at home in rock-gardens to give height amongst the ground grovellers and miniature bulbs. These plants need to be in scale with their surroundings and not swamp the other residents. Dwarf conifers will immediately come to mind and if they are selected carefully can indeed make ideal miniature trees for your mini mountain landscape. Do avoid spreading things like some of the junipers as what they lack in height they will more than make up for in spread, and beware of buying any others that just say 'dwarf' on the label without giving you any idea of what the label manufacturer means by the term.

Although dwarf conifers come in an amazing array of shapes and colours, their textures are usually similar as most have scaly or fine needle-like foliage. What else can we plant that will increase the variety for us? Dwarf rhododendrons are often suggested and these are fine as long as you garden in a cool climate and have an acid soil.

Many dwarf forms of usually tall deciduous trees have been discovered or developed that may have a place, such as *Ulmus parvifolia* 'Nire Keyaki', a tiny form of Chinese elm that will grow no more than about 20 cm (8 in) each way, or perhaps you may get a plant of Salix × boydii, a tiny miniature willow that in ten years will reach the dizzy heights of 15 cm (6 in).

A genus that rarely comes to mind is *Berberis*. There are over four hundred and fifty different species and who knows how many hybrids and cultivars. Most are medium to almost tall shrubs and even those that could be described as dwarf are often wide-spreading or, much worse, suckering. This habit is usually best avoided in rock-gardens, due mainly to the difficulty in extracting wayward suckers that have shot clean under a large boulder.

Most *Berberis* are decidedly prickly, hence the common name Barberries, and this seems in itself to discourage people from planting them. (They will, however, still fill their gardens with roses; what with pruning and flower picking, these need quite a lot of maintenance and are all too ready to fold us in their embrace). It is quite handy to have *Berberis* or something with a sting in its tail, or more accurately on its branches, that can be strategically placed to discourage cats, dogs and other people's children (one can train or yell at one's own offspring).

I have also noticed that ample precedents for including thorny plants in rock-gardens exist in full-scale mountains. Whilst bushwalking in the Southern Alps in New Zealand I often had to sidestep some very dangerous customers, like the huge and obvious Wild Spaniards (*Aciphylla colensoi*) or the equally spiky but less detectable Wild Irishman (*Discaria toumatou*). I was soon wishing I'd worn long pants.

Getting down to specifics, the particular *Berberis* I would like to discuss is *B. thunbergii* 'Helmond Pillar'. Just like the wild form, it is a hardy easygoing sun-loving shrub that will perform well even in rather poor soils. Unlike the wild species, it makes a more or less upright dwarf shrub rarely above 1 metre (3 ft). I might add that its varietal name could be a little misleading. Unless you are prepared to nip and tuck and tie in, you are more likely to end up with something rather more vase-shaped than pillar-like.

Having said that, I must point out that it will still make an interesting vertical accent shrub, ideal on corners, to define (as pairs) an entrance or as an unusual small tub specimen. *B. thunbergii* 'Helmond Pillar' could be worth

growing for its shape alone, but it has much more to offer. Its foliage starts out in spring as a rich deep burgundy colour, and this it holds until very late autumn, at least in my garden. The leaves then turn rich shades of scarlet and orange before shedding. It produces drooping spikes of tiny lemon-yellow flowers in spring and these can be followed by small bright red berries.

'Helmond Pillar' is but one of many varieties derived from this shrub, which is native to Japan. It has produced a range of burgundy forms, one with lovely gold leaves and some with unusual variegations. Most are too large and bushy for the rock-garden, although *B. thunbergii atropurpurea nana* (also known as *B. thunbergii* 'Little Favourite') makes a good dwarf bushy shrub with dark foliage. It is interesting to note that all *Berberis* have yellow roots and wood, not much use I know, unless you planted them upside down.

Brachyglottis repanda

Good foliage plants are at last gaining the attention they deserve. Perhaps the last time this happened was in that unfortunate phase we Australian gardeners went through in the 1960s when the hideous pebble garden was popular. Some of my older readers will probably remember the style. Lots of white quartz pebbles to blind you when the sun was shining, artistically placed chunks of red scoria and the mandatory tufts of black plastic poking through.

The poor unfortunate plants used in these moonscapes were bold architectural things like *Cordyline*, *Phormium* (New Zealand flax), *Cortadera* (pampas grass) and the huge spiny *Agave americana*, usually in the variegated form for extra colour. This style has all but disappeared, mercifully, and the few existing examples will usually be found adorning blocks of flats, with the more modern addition of empty drink cans and plastic shopping bags. Why, you may well ask, hasn't the National Trust registered one before they all disappear?

Is it any wonder that we have had to wait for a new generation of gardeners unfamiliar with pebble gardens to release some of these plants from the stigma so long attached to them. The *Phormium* species in particular have had a resurgence in popularity, due also to the release of many new colours and dwarf forms.

Also from New Zealand, but never to my knowledge afforded the dubious honour of pebble garden status, is the tropical-looking *Brachyglottis repanda*.

It comes from coastal and lowland forest up to 800 metres (2,600 ft) throughout the North Island and in the South Island as far down as Greymouth. In the wild it can make a small tree up to 6 metres (20 ft) tall but is usually only about 3 metres or so (10 ft) in cultivation. As it benefits from regular pruning and nipping to keep it shapely, you can easily keep it down to below 3 metres if you wish.

The large wavy-margined leaves (*repanda* means just that) can be 20 cm by 25 cm (8 in by 10 in) and in the wild species are soft green with a lovely felty white reverse. The form *B. repanda* 'Purpurea' has rich purple leaves, with their strongest colour in winter, as well as the white backs. This one was apparently discovered by a bushman (one W. Raymond) when he cut it down! Being observant he removed cuttings and these were later released to an adoring public.

These lovely leaves were once used as primitive postcards by the Maori tribes and even by early white settlers, as the white reverse will accept ink or pencil just like paper. It is known to the Maoris as Rangiora or Pukapuka and often less poetically to the white population as Bushman's Toilet Paper. I suppose it depends on what coloured bathroom you have as to which variety you would grow. The purple form should look too divine against lavender tiles. The leaves are supposed to be poisonous, but I assume one must eat them and not just use them externally for any problems to arise.

In spring it will produce large heads of tiny dirty white daisies that have a pleasant perfume, but these are of little account when compared with its stunning leaves.

Some authorities compare the scent to mignonette, just as well it doesn't smell like toilet cleaner. To grow it well, select a sheltered spot out of strong wind, which can damage the foliage. It must have a well-drained soil and once established can even cope with dry conditions. A little shade is also appreciated and this tends to encourage extra large leaves. In very frosty areas these slightly shaded aspects should also afford it some protection from the cold.

Until recently, the genus consisted of just *B. repanda*, its forms and a subspecies, *rangiora*, which has larger leaves. The taxonomists have been at work, however, and have included in this group the shrubby *Senecio* species, which means that we now have a genus of some thirty or so species.

The purple form of this admirable plant was given an Award of Merit in 1977 by the Royal Horticultural Society.

Buddleja colvilei

When Linnaeus (whose name was really Carl von Linné but who used the Latin form to match his vocation, which was after all to change every known plant name) gave a botanical name to the lovely Butterfly Bush, his spelling went a bit awry. The genus commemorates the Reverend Adam Buddle (1660-1715), who was an English botanist and in his spare time Vicar of Farmbridge in Essex. I wonder how many men of the cloth these days find the time to pursue such a consuming extra interest (I mean the botany not the soul saving).

The problem started when the plant was originally named by Dr William Houston. The obvious form is Buddleia, but he spelled it Budleia. Linnaeus accepted the name Houston had given to the plant, but spelled it Buddleja in his text and Budleja in the index.

The laws governing botanical names state that the first properly published name of a plant is that which it should keep. So even if the spelling is wrong, as in this case, it must stay, though many later experts have tried to correct it. The same holds for plants that get an inappropriate name, such as *Scilla peruviana*, which Linnaeus thought had originated in Peru, but is in fact native to the western Mediterranean region. As good as Linnaeus was, he wasn't infallible.

Buddleja is a comparatively large genus of at least one hundred species, which comes as something of a surprise to those who know only the classical *B. davidii* and its forms. It also has a wide distribution, extending from eastern Asia into South Africa and South America.

It is not (in my opinion) easy to select just one from this basically hardy quick-growing group of plants. They are nearly all good, ideal for quick screening and to give a new garden a well-furnished look in no time. If you select carefully they will give you colour all year round, as many flower in summer and even a few in winter when large shrubs are often lacking. I find them indispensable.

Most have a lovely honey scent ,which is a great bonus, and those that flower in the warmer months will live up to their common name (Butterfly Bush) and attract masses of these jewels of the insect world to enrich our gardens.

I have chosen *B. colvilei* to discuss here from my vast list of favourites, with I might add some regret that such beauties as *B. alternifolia*, *B. crispa* and *B. salviifolia* don't get a profile of their own.

Now getting to specifics, *B. colvilei* is a large more or less evergreen shrub to about 4 metres (12 ft) tall with strong upright trunks and slightly arching branches. Its individual blooms are the biggest in the genus. They are cherry-coloured flared trumpets with a white throat, some are 2 cm (1 in) long and the same across and look for all the world like a type of penstemon. They are produced throughout summer in slightly drooping panicles about 20 cm long and 8 cm wide (8 in by 3 in).

Its foliage is also good, being a deep grey-green and slightly woolly when young. The leaves can be up to 20 cm (8 in) long on a vigorous plant.

The plant is bushy enough to screen a view and yet not so dense as to exclude some light and air getting through, so it is ideal where you don't wish to feel too closed in.

Unlike many of its relatives it doesn't require butchering on a regular basis to keep it looking good, not that it won't handle it if you feel like doing so. Just spend a little time removing spent flower heads and occasionally cut out some older trunks to re-invigorate your plant. If it has a failing at all it may be

hat it doesn't ever seem to produce flowers in great abundance, but as it flowers over quite a ime I suppose we have to accept that we can't have it all ways.

Like most of the *Buddleja* genus, it requires nothing more than a well-drained sunny site, much like roses, for which I think it makes an admirable backdrop, particularly for those of a magenta persuasion.

This Himalayan shrub was named after Sir James William Colvile (1801-1880), who was a Scottish lawyer and judge in Calcutta from 1845 to 1859. I have often seen it spelt *colvillei*, with an extra 'l', but it wasn't named after Sir Charles Colville, who was Governor of Mauritius from 1828 to 1834.

It was discovered by Sir Joseph Hooker in 1849 and W. J. Bean's *Trees and Shrubs Hardy in the British Isles* suggests it is the handsomest of the genus; Sir Joseph himself even said 'the handsomest of all Himalayan shrubs'. I don't think I would go that far, but it is a good plant.

Bystropogon canariensis

What difficulties we create when we use common names! For example, when you ask for a lily do you mean a *Lilium*, or a *Hosta* (plantain lily), an *Ixia* (corn lily) or a *Gloriosa* or a *Littonia* (both called climbing lilies)? There are probably at least a score of quite different plants all commonly called lilies.

The only reason I mention this is to lead me into the subject of my next profile. If you came into my nursery and asked for a smoke bush I wouldn't immediately think of *Conospermum* (the Western Australian smoke bush) as I don't grow them in my damp climate. However, I might think of *Cotinus* from southern Europe, or *Bystropogon canariensis*, the Canary Island Smoke Bush. And this is the one whose praises I am going to sing.

Bystropogon is a medium evergreen shrub to about 2 metres (6 ft) if left unpruned or 1 metre (3 ft) if heavily cut back after flowering each year. It is inclined to become leggy so this is desirable.

The small grey-green leaves and the flower heads have a strong aroma when crushed or when you brush past; to me they smell very like pennyroyal, but you may disagree.

The plant produces its fluffy grey-green flower heads in summer and autumn, and these can be picked for the house as fresh material or even dried (a squirt of hair spray will help to hold the lot together).

Any sunny aspect and a well-drained soil should suit it and it would look at home in silver borders as well as in a cottage-style garden. I once saw one planted just outside the front door of a house and at night when the lights were on it looked like a luminous cloud, definitely making it easier to find the door.

It is easy to strike from cuttings so once you have it you needn't stop at one.

Camellia tsaii

Camellias could be said to be everybody's cup of tea. After all if it wasn't for *Camellia sinensis* we wouldn't be able to have a 'Piping Hot Cuppa' at all.

I must admit that apart from *C. sinensis* most of the commonly available camellias aren't my cup of tea. I find the *C. japonica* types as a whole rather boring and their dark green dense foliage oppressive.

The *C. reticulata* types usually have flowers of a ridiculous size reminiscent of those ghastly giant dahlias and the plants are often too sparse and gawky.

Sasanqua camellias manage well in avoiding the poor traits of most of the above with the added bonus of flowering in autumn, when they are most useful.

When I discovered some of the even smaller-flowered species of this large genus (some suggest it may be more than two hundred and fifty strong), I started to reappraise my somewhat negative attitude.

It is always risky to dismiss a genus when you aren't familiar with some of its lesser-known species. These are often far less gaudy than the better-known ones and this is the very reason why they aren't grown initially, as the vast majority of gardeners go for the big and blowzy.

Although I can hardly consider myself an expert in this field, having grown only a few of the species plus a few more of the perhaps thousands of hybrids, I have decided that my favourite camellia is the elegant *C. tsaii* from Burma, Yunnan and Vietnam.

If you know of one that is better after you have had me wax lyrical then please let me know as I'm sure I will want to grow it as well.

This species will grow to quite a size and has been recorded at over 10 metres (30 ft) tall. I would suggest that a 5 metre (15 ft) plant could be considered sizeable however.

Its branches are arching to pendulous and support rich green drooping leaves about 9.5 cm (4 in) long by 3 cm ($2^1/4$ in) across. The immature foliage is a charming coppery colour. Its leaves are also finely serrated and wavy edged, giving them a three-dimensional quality.

The flowers are indeed small for a camellia but are produced in profusion in the leaf axils during spring. In my plant they are pure white although some references suggest a pink flush on the outer petals. These tiny cups are also pleasantly fragrant, which is something that this genus is not renowned for.

I have found that it will regularly set seed that germinates freely around its parent so I usually have one or two to spare for friends who are also taken by its charm and elegance. Like most other camellias (excluding the reticulatas) it can also be propagated from cuttings without too much difficulty.

This species was introduced into England by George Forrest in 1924. It received an Award of Merit in 1960 and a First Class Certificate in 1985 when exhibited by the Savill Gardens as a shrub for a cool greenhouse. It will need no such protection in Australian gardens and if we treat it just as we would any other species or hybrid all should be well.

For those few of you who have not grown any camellias and need to have it spelt out, the following should suffice. Select a sheltered aspect with morning sun or semi-shade all day. Make sure that your soil is well cultivated with ample acidic compost and leaf-mould. Camellias resent very dry or overly damp conditions so it pays to be sure of good drainage and to give ample water in the warmer months.

With such an elegant plant pruning should not be necessary and may well ruin its shape

so restrict yourself to the removal of dead wood and allow adequate space for it to mature. If you wish, you could remove lower branches completely. This will then make your specimen more tree-like and thus save space to head height. To walk under a tall arching specimen is a delight.

Linnaeus named the genus after George Kamel. He was a Moravian Jesuit who lived from 1661 to 1706; like Linnaeus and many of his contemporaries he Latinised his name, to Camellus. He wrote a history of the plants of Luzon, in the Philippines, a place he had actually visited, which was quite something in those days. This treatise was published by John Ray in London in 1704 as part of his *Historia Plantarum*.

Carpenteria californica

Isn't it amazing how fickle we gardeners can be! How well I remember my first sighting of a flowering *Michelia doltsopa*. It was back in the mid 1970s while I was on a scholarship trip to New Zealand. I was just about blown away by its stunning white goblets, its upright presence, its rich leathery leaves and its superb scent. At the time, as an impressionable youth, I thought I had found the world's best tree. The other day I was driving through Toorak and I saw hedges of *M. doltsopa* behind white-painted walls all over the place. I yawned, and thought how commonplace they looked.

On returning home I felt a little self-psychoanalysis was needed, as many a good plant is condemned without good reason. Quite obviously, my reaction could be blamed on familiarity, but was there more to it than that? I have to say that to see one perfect specimen at its peak can mislead you into believing you have found the Holy Grail. If you take off the rose-coloured spectacles and look critically you will note, as most sellers of this tree will not tell you, that it will lose lots of old leaves in a far too obvious way just after flowering or, worse still, while in flower.

This is leading me to a completely unrelated plant. The only shared characteristics are a green and white motif and possibly Holy Grail status.

Carpenteria californica is a very handsome and hardy evergreen shrub to 2 metres (6 ft) or so. It has lovely white scented flowers with a boss of yellow stamens that sit clear of the rich green leaves and are produced in early summer, well after the spring display has waned. It enjoys poor but well-drained soil in a sunny aspect, with minimal summer watering in most areas; it will cope with but doesn't need regular pruning and will survive even the heaviest frosts with next to no damage.

If this very up-market relative of *Philadelphus* (mock orange) has a fault it is its habit of holding dead leaves in summer after flowering. I usually whip around my plant at this time, plucking, and hey presto! all is well.

You may ask why this highly desirable plant hasn't ended up as a hedge plant like *Michelia* and then fallen away from grace with discerning gardeners. The reason certainly isn't lack of public relations, as any book on shrubs from Great Britain will sing its praises.

The reason why *Carpenteria* isn't common is the fact that it is quite difficult to propagate. This fact can often destroy a good plant, because no nursery is going to promote something that they can't always supply and when it is available demands a premium price.

Carpenteria is a monotypic genus in the family Philadelphaceae (or Saxifragaceae or Hydrangeaceae depending on the authority you consult).

It comes, not surprisingly, from California and was named after Professor William M. Carpenter (1811-1848), an American botanist/physician from Louisiana. One could speculate as to which of his professions may have led to his early demise. It differs from most *Philadelphus* by being solidly evergreen, having a single style and a superior ovary (which doesn't mean that it produces more seed!).

If you can't cope with its botanical name, it is sometimes known by the rather contrived common name of Tree Anemone. It was discovered by Major-General John Charles Frémont (1813-1890) of *Fremontodendron* fame, an explorer and plant collector in western North America. It was first flowered in England by Gertrude Jekyll in 1885 and received a First Class Certificate in 1888.

With all these interesting characters in its history, and the fact that you could be the only one in town to own it, why aren't you hunting for one right now? It could almost be the 1930 penny of the horticultural world. But don't tell anyone else where you got it.

Catalpa bignonioides 'Aurea'

Catalpa bignonioides, commonly known as the Indian Bean Tree, is a most impressive shade tree. Its foliage is a lovely soft green and big and bold. The spreading limbs create a shady retreat in summer and its large panicles of white flowers marked with yellow and purple give it a truly exotic look. Even after the flowers are gone, its long green bean-like pods make an interesting conversation piece.

If it has a problem at all it is that due to its eventual size and the scale of its leaves it is usually too dominant for a suburban-sized garden. Everything around it will look insignificant and fussy, assuming they don't get swamped out altogether.

This hasn't stopped me from using a catalpa in my own not very big garden; it all comes down to how you manipulate the plant to suit your requirements and conditions.

To start with, I selected the gold-leafed form known appropriately as *C. bignonioides* 'Aurea'. This form is not as big-growing as its green-leafed parent so it could well be fine even if left to its own devices. It would, however, grow too large for the aspect I selected for it, which is as a centrepiece in my blue and yellow border. Even a small tree here would cast too much shade and swamp out the sun-loving perennials that are its bedmates. Besides, I wanted the foliage to stay more at eye level so as to sit amongst its companions and not high above them.

This is accomplished by the simple technique of coppicing, so that instead of a large tree I end up with a big bush. It takes no more than five minutes each winter to prune the strong canes produced the previous summer down to a permanent stump. In the first year, prune to about 30 cm (12 in) above ground, well above the graft. In successive prunings leave a little bit of the current year's growth, so that you have small stubs of growth from this year with fat little buds promising potential canes up to 2 metres (6 ft) or more in the next growing season.

I know that by doing this I am never likely to see a crop of its exotic flowers, let alone the intriguing pods, but throughout the spring, summer and autumn I will have its lovely soft golden leaves making a bold statement amongst my salvias and agapanthus and that is all I really want from it.

If I needed more height without things getting out of hand I would have pollarded my catalpa instead. By leaving a permanent trunk at a suitable height and pruning back to it each year a quite impressive standard could be developed.

What all this comes down to is manipulating plant material to perform the desired job in the garden. Just because a plant can grow to a large tree doesn't mean we have to let it. Gardening is after all a creative pursuit and the material we use can be made to do as we wish and not just left to get on with it. Once you can overcome your reticence and, like the Queen of Hearts, say 'Off With Their Heads' it can open up a whole range of possibilities.

Getting back to our catalpa, the other advantage of coppicing is that with the vigorous growth created by a combination of pruning and an established root system the foliage will be extra large and luminous, making it a far better foliage plant than it would otherwise be.

It isn't a particularly fussy tree and will grow quite happily in a range of soils. The foliage colour is best if planted in full sun and a little shelter from strong wind is advisable so that its leaves don't become ripped and tattered.

Catalpa bignonioides 'Aurea' has been in cultivation since 1877 and received an Award

of Merit in 1974 and an Award of Garden Merit in 1984.

So if you take my advice and plant one it may never be a 'Has Bean', or a 'Has Flower' for that matter, but it will be a 'Has Leaf' of great destinction.

Cavendishia acuminata

When I first started gardening I quite reasonably concentrated on plants that would not only grow but even flourish in my cool hill-station climate.

Why bother even attempting subtropical plants when I could grow dogwoods, Japanese maples and rhododendrons without even trying. My friends from warmer, drier climates were always green with envy when they saw plants flourishing for me that they would probably lose or, worse still, have languish for years looking like outpatients from a horticultural hospital.

However, as with most gardeners, I eventually realised that the world was full of wonderful plants I hadn't tried and who was to say that if I selected the right spot I couldn't have a frangipani or a stephanotis, plus a lot of fun extending the boundaries of what I could grow.

Before you start trying the impossible you need to keep in mind that you will often fail, so you need to be very philosophical about your losses and treat them as a learning experience. It is also important not to get carried away. It is far better to fill your garden with plants hardy in your region and just play with a few in non-strategic aspects that may or may not survive.

How you manage this material will have a great bearing on your success. Some easily propagated plants can be left through winter to live or die as the season dictates if cuttings are taken to over-winter.

Some things can be pot-grown so that they can be moved to a greenhouse or a sheltered verandah for winter protection.

I must admit that I often find it more attractive to have such plants in the ground than in pots, as they look more like part of the garden that way. To dig up and pot them each year is a bit of a nuisance so I have refined my techniques somewhat. I have a number of tropical plants, which I know I would lose planted, in large terracotta pots that are buried in the ground each spring after the frosts have passed. The mulch is then raked over the rims so they look as if they have always been there, much to the amazement of my horticultural friends, none of whom has realised my ploy.

One plant that is more likely to survive without such treatment but is none the less borderline for me is a lovely plant in the Ericaceae family, called *Cavendishia acuminata*. It comes from the mountains of Colombia and Ecuador.

It is often badly frosted even if planted in a spot that is cool and sheltered (its favoured aspect) but will usually shoot again from the base in the spring. Like most of its relatives it likes a compost-enriched acid soil that remains moist without getting wet, and shelter from hot winds and afternoon sun. In places like Melbourne, where frosts are rare, it should be easier than it is for me.

You could consider it as a container plant if soil conditions don't suit as its root system is comparatively small, so large flourishing specimens can be housed in a fairly small pot or even hanging basket. I always have one potted in reserve in case I get a really bad winter.

It can be grown as either a freestanding plant or a rambler. If it is not supported you can expect an arching, elegant shrub up to 2 metres (6 ft) but twice that height could be achieved if it is trained up something. Try it up a shaded wall or a post in a fernery and then its elegant trumpet flowers can be shown off to advantage.

I think it is an attractive addition to the garden all year round (frost allowing in my case) so deserves to be much more popular. The mature foliage is a really glossy rich mid-green topped in season by lovely coppery-pink

new growth so it could well be worthwhile for this alone.

Its waxy trumpet flowers are produced in terminal clusters during spring and early summer and are a glowing red tipped with white, something like some of the larger-flowered South African members of the *Erica* genus. After the flowers it produces a juicy blackberry-coloured berry (strictly a drupe), also attractive in its own way, although it is not edible as far as I know.

It is fairly easy to propagate from cuttings and will flower quite young so there isn't really any excuse for not having one. I only wish I could get some other species to try as there are supposed to be about one hundred of them. They probably aren't as hardy (which wouldn't stop me trying), and this may explain their absence.

This lovely and exotic-looking genus is named after William Spencer Cavendish (1790-1858), Duke of Devonshire and owner of Chatsworth House in Derbyshire.

Ceanothus arboreus

Australian gardeners are quite familiar with at least one of the cultivars of *Ceanothus* that is sold as *C.* 'Blue Pacific'. This isn't its real name but some enterprising nursery person renamed it to help with the marketing; it is certainly more evocative than the name with which it was originally christened.

I can't even remember what the old name was and I must admit that I don't much care. It isn't a plant I wish to have in my garden or my nursery.

One of my neighbours has however imposed one on me by planting it along our mutual boundary and the only thing I can say in its favour is that it is directly behind my blue and yellow border, so it fits into my colour scheme far better than if he had planted a pink camellia or a red rhododendron.

My objections to 'Blue Pacific' are as follows. It makes a large top-heavy spreading shrub that is hard to grow anything under. Its very deep green foliage is covered by its startlingly electric-blue flowers to such an extent that it tends to dominate any garden in which it is planted. I am usually quite happy with startling effects and blue flowers, but when this shrub flowers all the other denizens of the border pale into insignificance. Finally, at the risk of sounding like a snob, it is dead common so for me at least this is another nail in its coffin.

I wish that more Australian nurseries would consider growing some of the more elegant and refined *Ceanothus* species and cultivars. They are virtually without exception all hardy undemanding shrubs, requiring nothing more in our climates than a sunny well-drained site with perhaps a little shelter from strong winds, which may break limbs or even uproot large plants.

The only other considerations are that they resent disturbance, so make sure that you are happy with where you plant them as they don't like to be shifted, and finally they don't really like to be pruned back into old hard wood. If you feel they need cutting, do so regularly from a young plant (after flowering) so that only small thin branches need be touched.

If I was to grow only one variety (and there are many good ones) I would select *Ceanothus arboreus* 'Trewithen Blue'. This lovely cultivar was selected in Trewithen Gardens near Truro in Cornwall and has been given two accolades, an Award of Merit in 1967 and an Award of Garden Merit in 1984.

It will make a large shrub or even a small tree up to 4 metres (13 ft) or so with an open fan-shaped habit, never looking like a top-heavy mushroom and allowing ample light in around its base so that other plants will flourish at its feet.

The foliage is quite large, very glossy and not too dark a green, the perfect foil for its lovely flowers. Speaking of which, they are quite good-sized panicles of soft powdery blue, produced at least in my garden from mid spring into summer with an occasional spurt through into the autumn. As an added bonus they are also slightly scented; what more could you want?

As a shrub for the back of a border it is ideal or you could grow it as an espaliered plant up a wall. This technique is often recommended for *Ceanothus* in England as it gives them extra protection from the worst of the winter cold. Although our Australian winters are unlikely to have any effect on them they could still be grown like this to save room and to show them off in a different way than if they were freestanding. In very windy gardens a wall may be useful to preserve them from damage.

The name *Ceanothus* comes from the Greek

eanothos, a name used by Theophrastus for piny plants, which would seem to have little r no connection with the plants it has been pplied to. It is a genus of some fifty-five pecies and masses of hybrids, which are usually but not always evergreen.

If you are part of the gardening fraternity hat prefers common names you could call hem Californian Lilacs, although they are in he family Rhamnaceae (the Buckthorn family) and so have no real connection with the true lilacs. Nor are they restricted to California in the wild. They extend predominantly on the west coast from southern Canada to northern Mexico, where they often form a quite significant component of the vegetation, particularly in dry chaparral country and often in association with *Arctostaphylos* species. This suggests that they will do well in our often dry climates.

Cercis canadensis 'Forest Pansy'

I adore purple foliage plants. They have a place in almost every colour combination in the garden. Mixed with white and pink they give a rich effect that relieves the sweet sugary Barbara Cartlandish look that these colours on their own tend to create.

I have a border in my own garden that I have named after this famous romance writer. It is filled with pink and white old-fashioned roses and I have used such things as bronze fennel and burgundy berberis to great effect. I am also contemplating the introduction of black mondo grass as a border edge to simulate eyelashes to make the whole thing more authentic. I don't have any plant that resembles a Pekinese, unfortunately.

Bronze is also a good companion for rich colours like red, orange and yellow. It will create a sumptuous look reminiscent of old Persian carpets and allow even timid gardeners to incorporate and enjoy these often excluded tones.

However, some plants in bronze tones are to be shunned; the usually sombre light-absorbing foliage of the purple-leafed plums I dislike intensely. They create a black hole in the garden that I find thoroughly depressing and I often wish that local councils would stop filling suburban streets with these awful things.

You will find when you get hooked on burgundy leaves that the range is enormous and the different tones are almost as diverse as the shades of green obtainable in more usual leaves. Some are coppery brown, some almost black and others (those I usually use with the pink and white themes) have a rich claret red.

A plant I saw used regularly in English gardens that has started to find its way into Australian gardens is *Cercis canadensis* 'Forest Pansy', and a more beautiful burgundy foliage would be hard to imagine. The cultivar name at least for me seems quite inappropriate. It looks nothing like a pansy and is a bold and beautiful foliage plant that is no garden wimp.

It is related to the better-known Judas tree, *C. siliquastrum*, from the eastern Mediterranean, renowned for its masses of usually dark pink to magenta pea flowers. These are produced in quantity, often even on the trunks. With age it becomes a lovely gnarled picturesque small tree of a hardy nature, making it a useful specimen for even quite small gardens.

The common name is thought by some to indicate that this is the tree that Judas hanged himself from. Others suggest that the hanging woody seed pods may have given rise to the name, although they don't look that much like corpses. Probably the true origin of the name is that it is a corruption of Judea tree, as it was once common throughout that area.

Getting back to our plant, it is from North America and has no connection with Judas. Although its species name would suggest that it is from Canada, it is in fact native to the United States from New Jersey to Florida and is commonly known as Redbud.

It also produces small magenta pea flowers that can be used in salads or fried if you have a desire to do so. It isn't as showy as its more famous relative, but in the case of 'Forest Pansy' it isn't for its flowers that one is planting it.

The charming heart-shaped leaves are up to 12 cm (5 in) long and are a rich burgundy from the beginning of spring through until they drop. They are produced in quantity on a large spreading shrub, usually up to 3 metres (10 ft) or more. I suppose it could in time become a small tree but growth is slow enough not to cause undue worry about this and one can always resort to pruning if it gets delusions of grandeur.

It is fairly hardy and should grow in any vell-drained but moisture-retentive soil in sun r semi-shade with a good mulch over its oots. Plant it as a young pot-grown pecimen, as advanced ones don't usually ettle as well.

In my own garden I have created a harming combination (at least in my humble pinion) using 'Forest Pansy' with the lovely *Phalaris arundinacea* 'Feesey's Form' (or 'Mervyn Feesey'), a grass with beautiful silvery-white striped leaves to about 1 metre (3 ft), and that wonderful old hybrid musk rose 'Penelope', all bedded down in a silver carpet of lambs ears, *Stachys byzantina*.

I am sure you could think of many other ways of using the lovely *Cercis canadensis* 'Forest Pansy', so off you go.

Clerodendrum bungei

If I told you I had a wonderful plant that you just had to have, with leaves that smell like a Grand Prix track and with such incredible zest for life that it will sucker up metres from where it started, what would you do? Probably have me committed. I can hear you now, 'Poor Stephen, all those Latin names have gone to his brain'.

What if I told you I had this wonderful hardy shrub with handsome foliage and large clusters of highy scented rich pink flowers from mid summer till early autumn, and its common name is Glory Flower to boot? No doubt you'll be wondering why no-one has introduced it to you before.

The problem is that both of these descriptions apply to the one plant and I know which I would use if I was producing a printed label and wanted to sell some.

Our subject is *Clerodendrum bungei* syn. *C. foetidum*, from China and northern India, and for all its faults I hope to convince you that it is still worth planting.

It comes from a large genus of mainly tropical to subtropical shrubs, trees and climbers in the Verbena family and it is one of the few that can be grown outdoors in England. This doesn't mean that it's completely frost-hardy. In cold areas it is often cut to the ground by heavy frost but due to its capacity to sucker from the roots it can be treated like a herbaceous perennial and still bloom prolifically on the new canes that summer. If not cut by frost, it will grow to a branched shrub of 2 to 3 metres tall (6 to 10 ft), surrounded by its attendant suckers that can be left, removed and/or given to friends during winter. I just hope they stay friends!

Although the leaves do smell dreadful they look most impressive. They are large and heart-shaped, often as much as 23 cm (9 in) each way. The edges are nicely serrated and the petioles (leaf stems) and veins have a purple blush. Don't forget the fun you can have with unsuspecting visitors when you recommend they crush one.

When you have the chance to smell the large pink heads remember not to lean too closely, the smell of burning rubber will overpower the blossoms' sweet aroma. Even when the petals drop, the red calyx lobes can make an attractive feature.

Now we had better deal with this suckering problem. Of all the things a plant can do, suckering is the most likely to turn off a potential customer. I'm sure they have visions of bamboo thickets full of an invading army. I for one would rather deal with a few unwanted *Clerodendrum* suckers than have to mow a lawn, which must be done regularly and can take ages. A quick swipe with a spade or hoe will deal with the suckering problem, I know it's only temporary and will have to be done again some months later but how many jobs in the garden aren't repetitive?

Because of its upright habit of growth and the way it suckers you could find it useful planted in those narrow beds against walls, with a lawn or solid path to restrain its take-over tendencies. It is also useful as a background plant in a mixed border as it can be allowed to drift around and along the back, filling the gaps between more stay-at-home plants and giving a feeling of continuity.

Its cultural requirements are simple as you are more likely to wish to curb it than to have trouble establishing it. An aspect in sun or semi-shade will be fine. It is remarkably tolerant of different soil types and will even be quite happy in poor dry soil, which may just help curb it.

Prune older trunks out every few years if the cold doesn't do it for you, as this will invigorate and rejuvenate geriatric specimens.

It was introduced into England by Robert

·ortune in 1844 and received an Award of ⁄Ierit in 1926, presented no doubt by omeone who hadn't smelt its foliage.

The botanic name comes from the Greek *leros* ('lot', 'chance'), referring to the variable medicinal properties, and *dendron*, 'tree'. The species name *bungei* commemorated Alexander von Bunge (1803-1890), a Russian botanist. The synonym *foetidum* is self-explanatory.

Cornus 'Eddie's White Wonder'

One group of trees and shrubs for which I have a special fondness are the dogwoods, which are botanically known as *Cornus*, at least they are at the moment.

If some taxonomists have their evil way this highly ornamental genus may well be cut up into several genera, which will create some confusion and win them very few friends. All that will be left in *Cornus* will be *C. mas* and its close relatives. These produce small yellow flowers on the bare stems in late winter. Due to the fact that *C. mas* was the first species described it will have precedence over the more familiar large-bracted dogwoods, which will probably end up being called *Benthamidia* or *Benthamia*. These bracted species are the lovely flowering shrubs and small trees typified by the well-known pink dogwood, *C. florida rubra*.

Another group which have no petal-like bracts but small white flowers in flat clusters will become *Swida* or maybe even *Thelycrania*. A stately example of this lot would be *C. controversa* 'Variegata', the lovely tabletop dogwood. Finally the charming little creeping dogwood will be in another genus even though its flowers are bracted. Can you believe it will be known as *Chamaepericlymenum*? I can't see this name being readily accepted even by professional horticulturists, let alone home gardeners. I for one will always know it as *C. canadensis* and never *Chamae-thing-a-ma-jig*.

When you think about it, even the common name of Dogwood isn't a particularly flattering moniker, nor do things get any better when you find out that it came about because one species (soon to be a *Swida*) was used to make a wash for mangy dogs.

All this aside, I am so fond of the *Cornus* group that I now hold the collection, which consists of some forty species and cultivars, for the Ornamental Plant Collections Association. I do hope that it never becomes the *Cornus*, *Swida*, *Benthamidia* and *Chamaepericlymenum* collection even though I can see the sense in it all, just!

If by some quirk of fate I found myself in the awful position of having room for only one dogwood, it may surprise you to know that although I don't wish to think about such a fate I none the less know just which one I would opt for. Without a doubt the best all- round dogwood would have to be the hybrid with the dreadful name of *C.* 'Eddie's White Wonder'. Its pedigree is impeccable and consists of *C. florida* × *C. nuttallii*. These are two of the best species and the best characteristics of each were passed on to the offspring.

You can forgive the awful name to some extent when you discover the history involved. It was bred by Mr Henry M. Eddie, a nurseryman from British Columbia. He raised huge batches of this cross in the 1930s and 1940s and lost all of them bar one in a terrible flood in 1948. So it is indeed a Wonder in White from Mr Eddie's fields.

Obviously I am not alone in my love of *C.* 'Eddies White Wonder' as it received an Award of Merit in 1972 and a First Class Certificate in 1977. The Reginald Cory Memorial Cup was also awarded in 1973 (posthumously) to Mr Eddie for his achievement.

If you manage to buy a plant, which isn't easy due to some difficulties in production, you will wish to know how to grow it and what it does.

Dogwoods are usually best grown in the cooler parts of Australia and New Zealand, with an easterly aspect and shelter from strong winds. The preferred soil would be acidic and humus-rich, moist but well-drained and covered with a thick leafy mulch.

As the accompanying photo tells only a

mall part of the story I had best fill out the est of the details for those of you who have ne required conditions.

If well suited with soil and aspect *Cornus* Eddie's White Wonder' has remarkable ybrid vigour. My own specimen has topped metres (16 ft 6 in) in around ten years. It as now slowed somewhat and is putting nost of its energy into spread. Its branches re arranged in flat fan-shaped layers that ecome semi-pendulous with age. This of course means that even bare in winter its shape has something to offer. The huge 12 cm (5 in) white flowers are produced on top of the aforementioned branches in vast quantities during its mid to late spring season.

As if all this wasn't enough, in autumn its large curved leaves turn shades of scarlet, orange and burgundy. If you live in an area in which no self-respecting dogwood will flourish, all I can say is that I am very sorry for you.

Cotinus coggygria 'Royal Purple'

Shrubs that are brilliant performers from spring till autumn are few and far between and although I am the first to get excited by the ephemeral beauty of many garden plants like spring bulbs and flowering cherries I feel that garden space is too precious to be turned over to too many of these plants. In fact flowering cherries are something I prefer to get pleasure from in someone else's garden. After all, the flowering of cherries seems to stimulate Mother Nature into windy and wet tantrums, often making the show remarkably short term. That is assuming you get a show at all as in some areas possums and rosella parrots seem to relish the unopened flower buds.

My advice before you get carried away by a potted plant in flower or an alluring pictorial label is to ask some pertinent questions. Find out first if it has a long enough flowering period, check that its foliage is good enough when not in bloom (something that we don't often notice whilst waxing lyrical about its floral attributes) and whether it produces good berries or autumn foliage, or has attractive bark or form.

From the family Anacardiaceae (the Cashew family), which includes such diverse things as *Anacardium* (cashew), *Mangifera* (mango), *Schinus* (pepper tree) and *Toxicodendron* (the dreaded rhus), comes *Cotinus coggygria*, the Venetian Sumach or Smoke Bush.

This large shrub, which comes from Europe, the Himalayas and China, is hardy, quick-growing, deciduous and almost indispensable. During summer it produces fluffy pinkish plumes composed mainly of sterile flower pedicels that slowly turn smoky grey as they die.

In autumn the smoke turns to fire when its leaves turn brilliant shades of yellow, orange and scarlet.

As it can grow to about 3 or 4 metres (10 to 13 ft) it is almost a small tree and can be pruned to encourage that effect, making it a good specimen even in smallish gardens. Perhaps we could call it a shrub with delusions of grandeur.

In passing, it is interesting if not horticulturally important that the yellow wood (usually seen only during pruning) is used to make a high quality dye. It has also been known to cause dermatitis for some unfortunates rash enough to plant it. This I might add is very rare and only likely to affect those predisposed to such conditions who also prune the plant and have direct contact with the sap.

You might well ask how *C. coggygria* can be classed as a long-term brilliant performer. This is assuming that all summer and autumn isn't enough.

With this in mind we will move on to one of its varieties known as *C. coggygria* 'Royal Purple'. In the autumn colour stakes this one can be a bit of a fizzer but from early spring till late autumn it will flaunt its rich purple leaves and still give a reasonable show of smoke.

It normally grows to a shrub of only 2 metres (6 ft), and if foliage is your main aim it pays to coppice your plant every few years to obtain extra good colour. This will have a detrimental effect on the plumes the following year but we can't have everything.

If you can plant it where it will be back lit you will notice that it has a very fine red edge to the leaves, lovely at close quarters when covered with dew on early morning rambles.

This form originated in the nursery of Kromhout and Co. in Boskoop and received an Award of Garden Merit in 1984. I for one am glad they gave it a varietal name in English instead of Dutch, a very kind gesture.

If you don't want a purple-leafed form and would like the best autumn colour, I would

uggest *C. coggygria* 'Flame' and for the best lumes I would opt for *C. coggygria* 'Foliis urpureis', which is another larger-growing orm with light purple and green foliage and emarkable pink to grey smoke.

Just to finish off and use all my research, you may like to know that *Cotinus* comes from the Greek *kotinos*, which means 'wild olive' (goodness knows what that has to do with smoke bush), and *coggygria* is also Greek (*kokkugria*) and appropriately means 'smoke'.

Cyrilla racemiflora

If you are looking for a classy summer-flowering shrub that isn't too difficult to grow but isn't seen in every garden centre perhaps *Cyrilla racemiflora* is the plant for you. If its flowers don't start a chain-reaction these elegant drooping chains will create a favourable one with all who see it.

This large open-growing shrub will reach about 6 metres (20 ft) in favourable conditions and is semi-evergreen or semi-deciduous depending on whether you are an optimist or a pessimist. What leaves are shed turn rich yellows, oranges and reds in late autumn and early winter, giving the plant a second season of colour.

When the flowers die they are replaced by copper-coloured chains of tiny seed pods that look nearly as good as the live flowers. Not many plants I know of look as good with dead flowers as with live!

It has a wide natural distribution, extending in the north from Virginia and Texas south to the West Indies and to southern Brazil. This wide range would suggest that it will cope with various climates in Australia, assuming we have the right forms. I find it grows well in full sun with well-drained acid soil but in warmer areas a little afternoon shade is probably advisable.

It is quite easy to strike from summer cuttings and it will even send up an odd sucker that can be dug up to produce a new plant, so there really isn't any reason why it shouldn't be more available.

Cyrilla is a monotypic genus (only one species) in the Cyrillaceae family and was named after a Professor of Botany at Naples, Dominico Cyrillo (1734 or perhaps 1739-1799). It was introduced into Britain in 1765 and received an Award of Merit from the Royal Horticultural Society in 1901.

It is known as Black Titi, Leatherwood and Myrtle in its various native countries. As we use the last two names for quite unrelated plants I would suggest sticking to *Cyrilla*, which isn't really that difficult to say anyway.

If you would like a planting suggestion, why not use it as an overstorey plant to shade (but lightly) a bed of rhododendrons and azaleas. It will grow well with them and give summer and autumn colour when its companions are usually just green blobs.

Dacrydium cupressinum

When conifers come to mind we generally think of the pine, fir, or spruce forests in the mountains of the Northern Hemisphere. However, to my mind one of the world's most graceful and arresting members of this huge plant group comes from the cool mountain climate of New Zealand.

The plant in question is *Dacrydium cupressinum*, the New Zealand Rimu. For sheer elegance and form it is hard to beat.

Eventually, in its natural habitat, it becomes a forest giant to 60 metres (200 ft), but this should not discourage even those with a small garden from obtaining one, for its rate of growth is slow. It can even be grown in a large tub for many years.

Like the Tasmanian Huon pine, which is a relative, it was once prized for its durable timber, but due to excessive logging little of its timber is available today.

With a growth rate rarely exceeding 30 cm (12 in) a year and its liking for cool shaded aspects it can be recommended as a feature plant, either potted or planted in a fernery or under the canopy of larger deciduous trees. If potted it should be given a light root-pruning every few years and repotted with fresh potting mix; its potential life span in a tub can be substantially extended in this way. If after twenty years or so you can no longer cope and have to remove it or give it to a friend with a larger garden, you will have had good value from your initial investment.

To see its weeping fountain of drooping branches is something not forgotten.

The specimen in the photograph is growing in a Mount Macedon garden and stands about 12 metres (40 ft) tall after approximately fifty years, under ideal growing conditions.

Daphne genkwa

Some plants attain the stature of a Holy Grail amongst gardeners. Such things are usually very hard to get or difficult to keep once attained.

One such plant is *Daphne genkwa*, from China, the fabled Blue Daphne.

I must point out that it isn't really blue, more a rich mauve, but let's not let facts stand in the way of a good story. The blooms are quite large for this genus and are produced in quantity on its bare stems in late winter. Its narrow leaves are often bronze tinged whilst young and attractively set off the last of its flowers.

For the rest of the year it is an unremarkable twiggy shrub that can grow to about 1.5 metres (5 ft).

Two forms of this species are available (occasionally) in Australia, one with larger deeper flowers and long narrow leaves and another with smaller paler blooms and shorter leaves. If by some remarkable coincidence you are offered both, opt for the first. Although it tends to be the twiggier of the two it is by far the better flower. *D. genkwa* is hard to obtain due to the difficulties in propagation. I have had some success with semi-hardwood cuttings although you never know from one year to the next if you will succeed. The other technique suggested in books is to grow it from root cuttings. This is all very well but as many daphnes resent root disturbance there is a major risk to your stock plant.

The next problem that confronts would-be growers is where to plant it and how to care for it. Much of the information available in books is contradictory in the extreme. Some suggest shade, others full sun; some would have you believe that an acid soil is vital, others stress the need for lime. If gardeners try to follow all the advice, is it any wonder that *D. genkwa* is often said to be short-lived?

Perhaps if we look at its natural environment we will get some clues. It apparently grows amongst conglomerate rock and sandstone boulders on bare exposed hills, usually in full sun. I have found that it will grow quite well in an acid soil but an alkaline one shouldn't be a problem given its habitat. Full sun is quite important but the roots need to be kept cool under a thick mulch or amongst large rocks. Good drainage is also vital, so an open soil in a raised bed is the way to go.

Even if you have done all the right things this plant can still ungratefully die for no apparent reason; this of course only adds to the mystique amongst keen gardeners.

D. genkwa was first introduced into England by Robert Fortune in 1843 and he obtained it not from the wild but from a nursery garden near Shanghai. Apparently it died out (perhaps not enough summer sun?), and it was collected again in 1878 by Charles Maries for the great Chelsea nursery firm of James Veitch and Sons. This firm, which was an offshoot of the original firm in Exeter, employed an amazing array of distinguished plant collectors.

Few people bother with common names where daphnes are concerned, taxonomists take note. It is a shame that more plants haven't got such easy names, it would encourage more to use them.

Daphne was the name of a nymph, the daughter of the river god Peneius. She was apparently a comely wench of high virtue who attracted the dishonourable and persistent attentions of that god about town, Apollo. Zeus took pity on the poor distressed maiden and turned her into a shrub, which leads one to ask what he would have done if he disliked her.

If one can accept the concept of being shrubbed, it must be pointed out that it is more likely that Daphne was actually turned into a bay tree. These trees were once planted

at the entrance to the sanctuary of Apollo at Delphi and the foliage was used by his high priestess on ceremonial occasions. I hope it didn't make him mad having his face rubbed into his failure with Daphne.

Daphnes were once used medicinally, a fairly risky business due to their toxic properties. The berries of some species were used to violently relieve constipation and Gerard, commenting on its 'virtues', included purging phlegmatic humours, drawing water from the head and provoking vomit! The daphne was also used to induce abortion, so is it any wonder that Apollo lost interest.

Of the seventy-odd species of the genus *Daphne genkwa* stands out as a remarkable and different plant. It received a First Class Certificate in 1885 and has all the features to make it a connoisseurs' choice except for the fact that it is alas! not perfumed.

Dendromecon rigida

It is a shame that some plants never become as popular as they could just because they are difficult to propagate. But who can really blame the nursery trade, struggling to survive, if they prefer to grow easy well-known plants. After all if you can strike it in your hat, pot it up and sell it fast, life is so much simpler.

This attitude does lead to lots of problems for the keen gardener looking for something different. No nursery hoping to make a living is going to spend money promoting something it can rarely offer, so they all tend to grow the same old stuff. This in turn gives the retail customer that strange feeling of deja vu when going from garden centre to garden centre. It can quite easily become a vicious circle and in the end no-one wins.

So what can we do about it? I feel that the public needs to become more demanding, after all if a market can be seen to exist then some entrepreneur is bound to try and fill the void. Just remember that if you are wanting something rare and difficult you shouldn't quibble over price.

Nurseries already charge far too little for their produce and this does lead to lack of variety and poorly grown stock, so be prepared to pay for quality. No-one expects to pay a pittance for a Picasso. In nurseries as in other fields you get what you pay for.

Now that I've got my thinly veiled plug in for the true plantsman or woman's style of nursery as opposed to the supermarket garden centres, I suppose we had better move on to our plant in question.

Dendromecon rigida is a medium to large evergreen (or perhaps more correctly evergrey) shrub that can grow up to 3 metres (10 ft) tall, possibly the world's tallest poppy.

There is only one species, according to some reference books, or as many as two with one natural variety in others. *D. rigida* is however the only one that is ever likely to be stumbled on in Australia and then only occasionally.

It has stiff entire silvery grey leaves and these as well as its smaller yellow flowers separates it from its better-known relative, *Romneya*. For those poor unfortunates who don't know *Romneya*, it has large crepe paper-like white petals with a boss of yellow stamens. It is sometimes compared, with fair accuracy but no poetry, to a fried egg and has less claim to the common name of Tree Poppy than *Dendromecon*, as it is really a semi-herbaceous perennial. Besides, *Dendromecon* literally translates as 'tree poppy'.

Both *Romneya* and *Dendromecon* come from dry rocky chaparral in California and Mexico, so should be happy in any sharply drained sunny aspect. The soil shouldn't be too rich and I have known of losses due to over-kind owners being generous with manure.

Although this article isn't meant to be about *Romneya*, pretty well everything I recommend could be applied to both as their habits and requirements are basically the same.

Like many other plants of arid areas, the tree poppy has long questing roots and is resentful of any sort of root disturbance, which is a real pain to the propagator as the main technique is by root cuttings. When planting out don't tease out the root ball at all, just slide it into the hole and hopefully it will not notice. If you get it past this initial shock (and unfortunately there's no guarantee) then all should be well as long as you leave its roots alone.

Pruning consists of removing any old spent wood to allow room for younger shoots. This is best done in spring.

The cheery bright yellow poppies of *D. rigida* are produced throughout the warmer months and are lightly fragrant; its

ilvery foliage looks good all year as well as etting off the flowers to perfection.

It was discovered by David Douglas and ıtroduced into England by William Lobb bout 1854. William Lobb, who was a plant ollector for the Exeter nursery firm of James 'eitch and Son, also introduced *equoiadendron giganteum* (the Californian Big Tree). On an expedition in South America he discovered *Lapageria rosea*, Chile's climbing floral emblem, and he introduced *Tropaeolum speciosum*, the Scottish flame flower, which also hails from Chile but has so effectively clambered through the hedges in northern areas of the United Kingdom that they have claimed it for their own.

Desfontainia spinosa

When is a holly not a holly? When it's *Desfontainia spinosa*!

I regularly have customers ask me 'How much is that holly in the shade house, the one with the strange orange flowers?' Sounds a bit like a song title, doesn't it? I might even use it in my next album.

At first glance this shrub does have a more than passing resemblance to the English holly (*Ilex aquifolium*), with it spiny rich green leaves. This shouldn't be enough to trick those in the know, however, as the colour is a lighter green; also the foliage is arranged in opposite pairs, whereas the *Ilex* has leaves that alternate along its stems.

It is in fact in a quite different family called Loganiaceae. This family includes the *Buddleja* genus, to which *Desfontainia* has no passing resemblance. No wonder some home gardeners think that the botanists are pulling their collective legs. Some more reasonable botanists have suggested that it should be in the family Potaliaceae, which consists of a small number of genera from tropical and subtropical climates none of which I am familiar with, so that really simplifies things doesn't it!

Desfontainia is usually considered to be a monotypic genus although Mr. Bean (not of television fame, but W. J. Bean, author of the encyclopaedic work *Trees and Shrubs Hardy in the British Isles*) suggests that there are five species. Don't let this worry you too much as *D. spinosa* is the only one you are likely to encounter.

This plant is a native of the Andes from Colombia down to the Straits of Magellan. It was first described by Ruiz and Pavon in 1799 from material they collected in Peru. It wasn't until 1843 that it was introduced to Britain by William Lobb, who collected it in Chile, and it was also collected by Harold Comber in 1925-1926.

In the more northern parts of its range it is found growing in cool mountain cloud forests but further south it descends to sea level and can even be found on the islands of the Pacific coast.

In gardens it requires a soil of an acid nature that never dries right out and an aspect sheltered from hot winds and hot afternoon sun. Any position suitable for rhododendrons or camellias should be all right. I often recommend it as a companion plant for these as it flowers in summer and early autumn when they don't, thus extending the period of colour.

It is probably just as well that it doesn't bloom with them as the high proportion of pinks and cerise reds found in rhododendrons and camellias wouldn't blend happily with *Desfontainia*. Its waxy trumpet flowers are rich deep orange tipped will yellow and are usually produced in enough quantity to make a good show against the deep green leaves without being overbearing, and as it flowers for up to three months it certainly pays for its space.

The shape is normally fairly dense and this can be encouraged by a bit of trimming after flowering if you feel it necessary. As it is not a particularly fast-growing shrub it can even be used to good effect as a tub specimen.

A mature plant will usually be about 2 to 3 metres (6 to 10 ft) tall and about half as wide, although a remarkable specimen in Ireland was measured at 10 feet tall, 32 feet across and 118 feet in circumference. I'll let you convert it to metric as it sounds more impressive in imperial. I might add that the secateurs would have been in action a long time ago if this plant was in my garden.

If you are one of those fortunate people who love orange flowers and don't wish to stop at one *Desfontainia* but don't want to

purchase any more, it can be propagated with reasonable ease by cuttings taken in mid summer.

It was named in honour of René Louiche Desfontaines (1750-1833), who obviously wasn't around to see it in the flesh as it only came into cultivation ten years after his death. He was a French botanist who was a professor at the Jardin des Plantes, Paris.

It received an Award of Merit from the Royal Horticultural Society in 1931 and the form collected by Mr Comber and named after him (which doesn't seem to have reached Australian shores) received one in 1955.

So off you go and plant one, then when your next visitor asks about that strange holly with the orange flowers you can feel quite superior as you explain to this poor soul the subtle differences between these unrelated plants.

Dipelta yunnanensis

Few gardeners would not be familiar with the weigela, at least in its pink-flowered form with most unattractive (at least I think so) variegation. I have never been one that likes yellowish leaf colour and pink flowers together. Some may also know that you can get plants with white or carmine flowers and one with plum-coloured foliage (*W. florida* 'Foliis Purpureis'). Few know about the rare lemon-yellow species *W. middendorffiana* or the oddly attractive *W. coraeensis*, which has flowers that start white and deepen through pink to cerise before they shed, usually with every colour on the bush at once.

What everyone does know is that they are hardy, easygoing deciduous shrubs that are usually lovely in bloom but ordinary afterwards (variegations aside) and downright dead-looking in winter. I have no objection as a rule to deciduous shrubs, in fact most enthral me with their fat little buds with a blush of colour and full of the promise of things to come. But weigelas just look dead.

All this doesn't mean that I don't have any weigelas but I wouldn't use them as front of the border shrubs as their charms wane quickly after blooming.

I wouldn't, however, say the same for the more obscure but related genus *Dipelta* , which is also native to that Asian floral treasure-trove, China.

In flower it could very well be mistaken for a weigela with its soft pink trumpet flowers, but of the four known species only two, *D. floribunda* and *D. yunnanensis*, are likely to be obtainable (after exhaustive searching) in Australia.

Of the two I favour *D. yunnanensis* even though the blooms on the other are larger; the colour is much the same and I think *D. yunnanensis* is the more graceful of the two. They are, however, quite similar and I would be happy with either (but not both) in a small garden.

Before I get too specific I will mention that *Dipelta* is a genus of hardy deciduous shrubs, usually to 4 metres (13 ft), whose only requirement is a well-drained but not deadly dry soil in a sunny or semi-shaded aspect.

D. yunnanensis produces masses of softest pink trumpets attractively marked with orange in the throat during mid to late spring. By this time its leaves are well developed and they have a fresh lush greenness and poise that *Weigela* cannot match.

As the first flowers fade the major difference between the two genera becomes apparent. *Dipelta* produces lovely green flat papery seed pods very like those of an elm; these pleasing appendages slowly turn from green to copper by late summer and give something to enjoy in all the various colour changes. They are quite large and are produced in quantity so can make a subtle impact and also an interesting addition to a bowl of flowers.

All this would be enough for me to opt for *Dipelta* over *Weigela* as a rule but it doesn't stop there. The leaves turn a lovely pale yellow in autumn, as good as any weigela, and in winter instead of looking like an upright pile of dried kindling its branches show some copper-coloured bark that usually peels back in strips, a most satisfactory winter effect.

D. yunnanensis usually has fairly upright primary stems. The smaller secondary twigs spread out, so that although it is of a somewhat upright habit it is never stiff. *D. floribunda* is usually more spreading than *D. yunnanensis*.

Both can be pruned, usually by completely removing the oldest canes every so often, but avoid this except in necessity as they tend to be more floriferous on unpruned specimens.

Unlike so many of the shrubs I have written bout, *D. yunnanensis* seems never to have eceived an award or accolade of any type. I an only assume that no-one has thought to isplay it for one, and not that it is ndeserving.

Dipelta comes from the Greek *di*, meaning 'two', and *pelte*, 'a shield', which alludes to the shield-like seeds. The species name of *yunnanensis* of course means that the plant comes from Yunnan province in China. It was introduced from there in 1910 by George Forrest and originally discovered by Abbé Delavay in 1886.

Disanthus cercidifolius

Autumn at least in southern Australia is probably the most congenial time of the year. The dry heat of summer is behind us, the weather is usually stable and we don't get as much of that blustery wind so typical of spring. It is definitely a time to get out and enjoy our gardens. So I think it makes good sense to plant for colour at this time of the year.

We also know that winter is just around the corner so it pays to make this season as cheery as possible, so that at least for a while we can ignore the inevitability of the wet and cold to come.

Many plants that we use for autumn colour add little to the garden during the rest of the year but we still use them regardless. I am normally the first to object to one week wonders but when it comes to autumn coloured foliage I will usually ignore my own advice.

In a country like Australia, where our native flora is almost invariably evergreen, it is easy to end up with a garden that changes little throughout the yearly cycle.

Without dramatic weather changes like snow in winter, if you were suddenly transported into a fully evergreen garden on a sunny winter's day (they do occur) you might find it hard to pick the season.

If you plant some deciduous things around, you will then know it is winter when they are bare, spring when they break into leaf and autumn when their leaves turn brilliant shades.

This leads us back to autumn foliage again. Part of the charm and sometimes frustration of autumn foliage is that from one year to the next the same plant can vary considerably in colour and timing. For those who open their gardens for public inspection it can be quite nerve-racking watching and waiting to see if you picked the right date this year. It might even pay to have a sign made telling people they should have seen it last week!

I am often asked to name my favourite (or even worse 'The Best') autumn-colouring plants. In a climate like the one I garden in this could well be a very long list. Having said all this, a plant that must certainly come close to the top of my imaginary list would have to be the lovely *Disanthus cercidifolius*, from China and Japan. Before you read further I must add that it wouldn't make it in a catalogue of easy and foolproof plants.

To start with I will quite unfairly whet your appetites by discussing its beauty and then bring you back down to earth with a bang when I discuss its requirements.

It makes an elegant multi-trunked large shrub, rarely exceeding 3 metres (10 ft) in height. The twigs arch out in a most satisfactory way so that during the winter it has a pleasing silhouette. During its dormancy it produces its quaint little burgundy starfish-shaped flowers that sit back-to-back on short stems. These certainly lack size so won't make an obvious show, but we aren't growing *Disanthus* for its flowers anyway.

From spring until autumn it is covered with lovely heart-shaped blue-green leaves. The foliage has more than a passing resemblance to that of the Judas tree, *Cercis siliquastrum*, hence its species name *cercidifolius*.

It is in autumn that *Disanthus* shows its true glory. The leaves towards the centre of the plant that get the least light will usually go clear yellow. Those a little further out will turn shades of orange, and those on the outside will exhibit leaves in tones from scarlet to deepest burgundy. With just this one plant you can have all the autumn colours.

Now we had better mention the down side to *Disanthus*. It requires a cool sheltered aspect well out of reach from the hot summer winds, plenty of light without the direct

fternoon sun and a humus-rich acid soil that never wet or dry.

Mulch it well to protect its surface roots and ho knows, you may end up with a plant that ill turn all your friends green with envy.

As a companion for dwarf rhododendrons nd azaleas it is excellent. Its shape and foliage ill make a lovely change and its autumn olour will enliven the bed when its bedmates are often no more than rather dreary green mounds.

It was first introduced into cultivation in 1893 but even in England it is still considered unusual. An Award of Merit was given to it in 1936, the first such award for autumn foliage, and in 1970 it gained a First Class Certificate. All in all, it is a gem of the Hamamelidaceae (Witch-hazel) family.

Dorycnium hirsutum

It seems to me that many gardeners are still rather unfortunately filling their gardens with masses of silver foliage and lots of pale shades in flowers. A profusion of pale flowers and silver foliage is of course very safe, highly tasteful, and perhaps soft and romantic. It is however rarely thought-provoking, stimulating or exciting.

Many people see such subtle gardening as exuding 'Olde Worlde Charme', but I wonder what era of the old world they are alluding to, it certainly wasn't the nineteenth century era of carpet bedding and lava-flow rockeries. Victorian gardeners often showed a remarkable exuberance in their colour combinations, which is understandable when you remember the amazing variety of new plants constantly being introduced in that period. Why not splash out with all those brilliant colours when they became available?

Of course I enjoy using plants with silver and grey leaves in my garden but I have never had a love of the silver border. I use them sparingly as contrast plants amongst things with more classically green foliage. When I do use them I prefer to contrast them with strong-coloured flowers such as magenta in preference to white or pastels, which tend to disappear into them.

In the supposedly softer light of an English garden a silver and white border may well look luminous, whereas in a classically hot dry Australian summer such a border tends to look like the weather, hot and dry, rather like mallee scrub. In such gardens during such weather I am always looking for some rich dark cooling green to lower the temperature of my mind if not my body.

Now if you are still determined to stick with silvers and greys, at the risk of reinforcing your attitude I would like to discuss a plant with pastel flowers and silvery foliage that will be a boon to your romantic subtle borders.

Dorycnium hirsutum is a member of the Pea family (Leguminosae); it is in a genus of some twelve species consisting of sub-shrubs and herbs found in the Mediterranean region and the Canary Islands. My selection is the only one I have grown so I can't speak for the ornamental qualities of the others.

Like the vast majority of silver-foliage plants, *D. hirsutum* requires nothing more than an open, sunny, well-drained aspect. This shouldn't be beyond most of us.

It will quite quickly grow to about 1 metre (3 ft) tall by about as wide, making a reasonably solid dome of foliage, and the only regular care required is to occasionally remove older spent wood.

In cold areas it can become semi-deciduous but will usually hold enough foliage to keep it looking reasonably respectable throughout the year. Its silvery-green leaves are slightly woolly and are divided into three leaflets.

It produces its pale pink to white pea-shaped flowers (this means its flowers are shaped like those of a pea not like a pea pod!) in terminal clusters throughout the warmer months.

These are followed by attractive coppery-coloured clusters of pods that look very little like those of peas. These seed capsules are quite ornamental in their own right so this amenable plant certainly pays for its space.

You may even like to use *Dorycnium* as an alternative to lavender or rosemary as an informal low hedge. It doesn't attract as many bees as they do, so this could be something of a relief if you need to walk past it regularly.

A hedge would of course require a number of plants so if you can't afford to buy the lot, just get one to start and collect its seeds in

ıutumn to be sown the following spring. This ›hould give you ample young ones to be ɔlanted out the next autumn.

For a plant that has been in cultivation since 1683 it is too rarely seen. Perhaps it will one lay be given an award to push it along. I hope n the meantime my little essay may improve its profile.

Finally, its botanical name comes from the Greek word *doryknion*, which was apparently the name of a convolvulus. It was later, for no apparent reason, transferred to this genus. The species name *hirsutum* obviously means 'hairy' so at least this is appropriate.

Drimys winteri

Are you looking for a beautiful plant and don't mind a challenge? Read on.

Drimys winteri is a charming evergreen large shrub or small tree from South America that botanists sometimes place in the family Magnoliaceae, or in the small family Winteraceae.

The generic name means 'acrid', alluding to the bitter taste of its bark, and the species name commemorates Captain Winter, who sailed with Sir Francis Drake. He collected the bark to use as a treatment for scurvy amongst his crew. I can find no record of it being successful, but as most gardeners don't have such a bad diet it probably isn't necessary to find out. One can always eat an orange and it will no doubt taste better anyway.

Before I point out the attractions of this plant I must warn you of the problems. Winter's Bark, which is the common name, has a well-deserved reputation for being difficult to establish. Even if it has ideal conditions it may still not like you and will suddenly and dramatically die. If it produces new growth, all will probably be well.

As for growing conditions, select a site with well-drained acid soil with plenty of organic matter, facing into the morning sun. Mulch well after planting to keep the roots cool, and make sure it gets ample water in summer. It will wilt and shed leaves quickly if it isn't damp enough, but after a good drink will stand upright again overnight.

After all this, why plant a *Drimys*? It has large bright green leaves that smell peppery when crushed. These are attached to reddish-coloured stems and in late spring it produces large umbels of ivory-white star-shaped blooms.

The flowers are supposed to be well scented (all the books say so) but mine is either a scentless clone or my nose doesn't work. Even if it had no perfume I wouldn't be without my tall, elegant plant of *D. winteri*, which looks so good growing near rhododendrons and similar plants.

In the six years mine has been planted it has shot up to about 5 metres (16 ft 6 in) and has flowered for the last three years.

So if you are undeterred, go out and buy a young plant; it should be easier to establish and won't have cost so much if it doesn't grow. You just might be the envy of your neighbours.

Edgeworthia chrysantha

Edgeworthia chrysantha (also known as *E. papyrifera* and commonly as the Yellow Paper Daphne) is a charming deciduous shrub from China that grows to about 2 metres (6 ft) and isn't often seen in this country. I hope the following description may tempt you to try it.

It is a relative of the true *Daphne* in the family Thymeleaceae, so its common name has some applicability. It requires similar growing conditions, that is a moist but well-drained soil and an aspect where it is exposed to morning sun but sheltered from summer heat and hot winds. Its only real affliction seems to be slugs and snails, which will climb right to the top of the plant to eat its foliage and more importantly its growing tips. I have had young specimens destroyed by their attentions when I was off my guard.

The daphne-like flower clusters are produced on the bare twigs in late winter. They are a soft yellow colour with white fur on the outside of the tube. Although they are slightly scented don't expect too much. Its leaves are quite large and pale green throughout the season, pleasant if not exciting.

The shrub has an interesting vase-shaped habit. As it grows, the new branches almost always grow in clusters of three so it will have a clean trunk broadening up higher, leaving ample room to underplant with small bulbs and perennials.

A particularly attractive effect could be created by planting at its feet a drift of lemon primroses to echo the colour of the *Edgworthia*, or perhaps you could try a few clumps of dark burgundy *Helleborus orientalis* hybrids, both of which would be in flower with their larger companion.

Although this plant is native to China it has long been cultivated in Japan, where its tough stringy bark was used to produce high-quality paper on which the yen was apparently printed, hence the title of this profile.

Because the flowers are just too lovely not to pick for a vase a warning is in order. Make sure that you do not try to snap a twig as you are likely to strip the bark right back to the base of the plant, something neither it nor you will enjoy. Always cut them with sharp secateurs and watch out when friends are just helping themselves to a piece.

Two other varieties are sometimes met with that you may like to try. The first is *E. chrysantha* forma *rubra*, generally sold as 'Red Dragon' in Australia. This one has the same habit as the species but the flowers are a strong shade of orange. Perhaps you could underplant this one with an orange trumpet narcissus for an interesting effect.

The other one sometimes met with is *E. chrysantha* 'Grandiflora', which is the typical yellow colour but has larger heads and more upright-facing flower clusters. Its leaves are also bigger and its stems are thicker and more rigid. It almost (but not quite) looks like a dwarf frangipani in its shape. These heavier branches may not be to everyone's taste, but it will certainly make a good conversation piece.

All in all I think that I would usually opt for the wild form as it is more graceful than 'Grandiflora' and a more subtle colour than 'Red Dragon', even though I am not renowned for my subtlety.

The genus was named after Michael Pakenham Edgeworth (1812-1881), of the East India Company. He was a keen amateur botanist and collected many new plants in India during his time off from his usual duties.

The species name *chrysantha* means 'with golden flowers' and *papyrifera* means 'paper-bearing'. Some authorities suggest that this second name belongs to a slightly different

species and isn't a synonym for *chrysantha* and that the true plant has whitish blooms. If this is the case I want one!

A third species from Nepal and Sikkim that is also sometimes listed is called *E. gardneri*. It is said to have flowers that are white, stained yellow, which doesn't sound as if it is all that distinct either, although it must be admitted that a dry botanical description often leaves out much useful horticultural information.

Embothrium coccineum

One of the glories of the South American Andes must surely be the breath-taking *Embothrium coccineum*, commonly known as Chilean Fire Tree.

It was first discovered and named when James Cook was on his second voyage, and when it is in flower you would have to be blind to miss it.

There are some eight or so species of this South American genus and *E. coccineum* itself has several forms from different latitudes recognised throughout its range. Some are tall slender evergreens from lowland forests, whereas others can be smaller semi-deciduous shrubs that come from higher altitudes or lower latitudes.

The form usually grown in Australia is solidly evergreen and can reach heights of 7 to 8 metres (23 to 26 ft). It is usually quite upright in shape although it has a tendency to sucker and these often come up quite some distance from the parent tree. The suckers are easy enough to deal with if you don't want them or they can be lifted and potted as presents for friends.

This suckering habit is unusual in the Protea family, in which *Embothrium* is included; even more unusual is the fact that the suckers can be lifted and survive, as this family is renowned for its resentment of disturbance. New plants can also be struck from semi-hardwood cuttings.

Like the rest of the family it dislikes strong manures or phosphate fertilisers, so give it no more than rotted compost and a good thick layer of leaf mould as a mulch. The mulch will keep its roots cool in summer and as long as your soil is deep and acid and the aspect isn't too hot and dry in summer you may well be able to grow it. This of course means that it won't grow well in many areas of Australia and will probably only flourish in the hill-station gardens in places like Mount Macedon and the Dandenongs in Victoria, the hills near Adelaide, the Blue Mountains in New South Wales and of course several locations in hilly parts of Tasmania.

If you can grow rhododendrons well, ignore the above and have a go anyway.

Having got a plant established things should start happening fairly quickly. My specimen was more than 3 metres (10 ft) tall in about four years and started to flower in its third year. It is now after ten years a well-clothed tree about 4 metres (13 ft) tall. The upward growth has now slowed down somewhat, but specimens have been recorded in south-western Ireland that exceed 15 metres (50 ft). This isn't likely to happen in our usually drier climate but if it does get out of hand (lucky you!) then you could always cut it down and it will be off and away again from the stump. The wood, which is apparently beautifully marked, could then be dried and used for wood-turning. Think how impressed your visitors would be with your *Embothrium* candlesticks!

The brilliant spidery orange and scarlet flowers are produced for about three months in spring and nectar-feeding birds find them even more attractive than the average grevillea, which is probably their usual fare. If this colour is too much for you then you can live in hope that some day someone will import the yellow or white forms that are known to exist. I know I would like to have them but I would still keep my scarlet one. Those lucky English have got the yellow, although I don't know how available it is there.

Its leaves are pleasant all year round, being a rich mid green and nicely netted with pale veins. On a vigorous specimen they are about 18 cm long by 3 cm wide (7 in by 1¼ in).

Embothrium coccineum was first introduced into England by William Lobb in 1846 and it received an Award of Merit in 1928.

The form usually grown here is probably of the Longifolium group and although these more evergreen forms are less cold-tolerant in England it received a First Class Certificate in 1948. The more deciduous Lanceolatum group gained the high accolade of an Award of Garden Merit in 1984.

Finally, its botanical name comes from the Greek words *en*, which means 'in', and *bothrion*, which is a little pit. This alludes to the fact that the anthers are sunk into pits in the calyx. Not one of its more outstanding features, I would have said.

Enkianthus campanulatus

This article is directed to all of you out there that have a passion for and grow loads of rhododendrons and azaleas (which are of course botanically in the *Rhododendron* genus anyway). The vast majority of them, particularly the hybrid rhododendrons and evergreen azaleas, make a wonderful show whilst in bloom. But have you ever noticed how stodgy and heavy the foliage can be, and how lacking in form and grace a bed full of them usually is once the spring is past?

A mass of these plants can be if not depressing at least very ordinary for a good part of the year and if you are blessed with the climate and acid soils in which they flourish it is so easy to get carried away and plant far too many.

Many of you are by now probably quite offended and ready to leap to the defence of your beloved shrubs. Others may be cheering, but gardening is after all a matter of taste and so it should be. I find that any garden with a preponderance of one genus tends to look more like a collection of stamps than a well-thought-out garden. It may well be fascinating to other collectors but usually doesn't make a good landscape.

If you are still determined to have more varieties than anyone else so be it, but perhaps you might like to give some thought to planting companions with them that will enhance your garden's appeal and give the eye something else to stimulate it.

Plants with airy grace and form like Japanese maples spring to mind as suitable bedmates. Their shapes, forms and foliage colour, particularly in autumn when rhododendrons can be looking tired and dusty after a long Australian summer, can give the garden a real lift. A less well-known but equally useful group of shrubs ideal to mix with them are the *Enkianthus* species.

This smallish genus of some ten species hails from the Himalayas to Japan and all have a distinctly oriental look, which is appropriate considering their origins. They are virtually all deciduous shrubs that vary in height and spread depending on the species you select and are all without exception worth having. With such a small number to select from it is un- likely that they will then become a dominant collection in any but the smallest of gardens.

Because they also come from the same family (Ericaceae) as rhododendrons they like the same conditions and have the same fibrous root system that won't compete unduly with their more famous relatives. Probably the best species to select if you are limiting yourself to one is *Enkianthus campanulatus* or the very similar *E. deflexus*.

The habit of growth is for me one of the major assets: both are tall narrow shrubs that under ideal conditions may exceed 4 metres (13 ft) but are usually seen up to 3 metres (10 ft). The narrow habit is a charming break from the more usual dumpy bushy growth of the rhododendrons and the *Enkianthus* are unlikely to shade or compete for space with them.

The lateral branches of *Enkianthus* are arranged in lovely tiers that show off the pendulous flowers to perfection and look good even when the shrub is bare in winter. Such a habit means that they take up little room and will add much-needed height even in narrow beds or between windows to soften the house walls without blocking the view. They can also be used as an exclamation mark at the end of a bed, or as a pair of sentinels on either side of a path to lead one's eyes in the right direction. The difference between the two species mentioned is that *E. campanulatus* has bell-shaped flowers as the name suggests, and *E. deflexus* has petal tips that reflex a little. Not enough difference for me to say one is better than the other.

E. campanulatus is probably the most vailable species so from here on in I will oncentrate on it.

In spring the flowers are produced in drooping clusters below the branches, with a base colour of creamy-lemon overshadowed by the rich deep pink veining in the petals, so that they are usually described as pinkish. Its soft green foliage comes into its own in utumn when it usually turns shades of ellow, orange and red before shedding, making it an attractive plant at all times and a really good thing in both spring and autumn.

This Japanese species was first introduced by Charles Maries (1851-1902) for James Veitch and Sons' Chelsea nursery in 1880. It received an Award of Merit in 1890 and an Award of Garden Merit in 1984.

Its unromantic name is derived from the Greek words *enkyos*, which means 'pregnant', and *anthos*, 'a flower', alluding apparently to the swollen corolla of some species.

Escallonia bifida

It is part of the perversity of human nature to think that if something is too easy it can't be worth having. This applies as much to plants as it does to everything else in life.

A plant or genus of plants can be damned with faint praise when described as hardy and useful instead of demanding and spectacular.

If a whole genus is described as useful but has one member of outstanding merit, that plant is often overlooked, much to the detriment of our gardens.

One such genus is *Escallonia*, whose species seem to be far more appreciated in England, where they aren't considered as solidly hardy as here in Australia, where they are almost indestructible.

I know that if I suggest them to my customers I am likely to get one of two responses. If said customer is an experienced gardener I will get 'Not one of those common old things'. If they are people who happen to own land because they have a house, and wish only to fill the garden with easy plants, I will hear 'I will have one, two or many of those'. Of course customers in the first group will look down their noses and suggest that the others know no better, which in a way is true.

For many years I considered escallonias to be beneath me and didn't even bother stocking them for sale. Although I would hardly say I've done a complete reversal I now propagate three species. Needless to say I've selected what I consider to be the best of the forty or so species in existence. Funnily enough my selections at least at this stage don't include any of the multitude of hybrids available.

As far as I am concerned the supreme species is *Escallonia bifida*, from southern Brazil and Uruguay. It was once called and is sometimes still listed as *E. montevidensis*, after Montevideo in Uruguay. It is something of a relief when a new name is given that is easier to say and spell than an older one, it is usually the reverse.

So what is so good about this shrub that sets it apart from the rest?

It isn't its foliage that excels, the leaves of *E. laevis* and *E. pulverulenta* (the other species I grow and sell) are much better. It is however attractive enough, being a rich mid green and about 10 cm long by 2.5 cm at its widest point (4 in by 1 in).

Speed of growth is a consideration and our selection can keep up with the best of them. After a quite short space of time you will have a large evergreen shrub or small tree to 5 metres (16 ft 6 in) tall, making it an ideal choice for screening or as a background plant in deep borders. If anything it can grow a bit too fast for its own good as I regularly have branches snap in the wind. I don't, however, lose sleep over it as they are soon replaced.

Like the rest of the genus, *E. bifida* is tolerant of drought, salt, lime, and infertile soils; so long as you don't mind having an easy life, plant one.

It is in late summer and autumn that the escallonias flower and this is when *E. bifida* really stands head and shoulders above its relatives.

The individual blooms are tiny pure white trumpets with a green eye and are produced in large panicles that can regularly exceed 15 cm (6 in) in length. I have even measured them at over 20 cm (8 in). This I try to do when no-one is about, you always get odd looks if caught flower measuring.

I like to use the flowers indoors and find they last well when cut. If I don't manage to pick them all, which isn't likely, I then lightly prune after their season to tidy up. This is only for aesthetic reasons as I have seen completely unloved specimens flowering their heads off.

It was introduced into England in 1827 and eceived an Award of Merit in 1915 so it's een around a while but is rarely met with in ardens here even though its less attractive elatives are often seen.

So at least until you have all planted one on my recommendation it could still be considered worthy for its rarity as well as for its hardiness and summer-autumn show.

Eucryphia cordifolia

Do you, like me, collect plant trivia? I not only have an unquenchable thirst for all pertinent and useful information such as country of origin or soil types preferred but I also have a love of useless facts surrounding any plant.

Isn't it exciting to know that a plant was once used in witches' potions or was discovered by some famous person? Better still if it was named after a colourful character, or somebody fell to his death trying to collect it.

I find that the more I know about any given plant (both practical and trivia) the easier it is to remember the name, where to plant it, how tall it grows and so on. It also opens up limitless avenues of research for the inquiring mind. Most importantly, for me, it gives my plants a personality.

This is all leading me to a favourite group of plants that would seem to support the theory of continental drift and trace their history back to the misty past in Gondwanaland. The genus in question is *Eucryphia*. It contains only five species, two of them from Tasmania (*E. lucida* and *E. milliganii*), one native to New South Wales and Victoria (*E. moorei*) and two from South America (*E. glutinosa* and *E. cordifolia*). Probably the best known in Australia is *E. lucida*, which is commonly called Tasmanian Leatherwood and is the plant from which bees make the famous strong-flavoured honey.

It is, however, *Eucryphia cordifolia* that I wish to discuss here.

Like both the Tasmanian species, it is a large upright evergreen shrub or tree with rich deep green foliage, and like all of the other species it produces its lovely blossom in late summer. Each flower is about 5 cm (2 in) across and is superbly set off by its boss of lemon stamens.

If given a cool aspect and acid organic soils it will grow into a tall plant perhaps as much as 5 metres (16 ft 6 in).

All the *Eucryphia* species are useful as companions for plants such as rhododendrons, as they not only enjoy the same conditions but flower when the rest of the bed can look pretty ordinary.

Now to finish off with a little more trivia. *E. cordifolia* was introduced into England in 1851 and received an Award of Merit in 1936. The genus name is from the Greek *eu*, meaning 'good' or 'well', and *kryphia*, meaning 'a covering'. It refers to the cap-like cover formed by the calyx.

P.S. Since first writing this profile in 1997 a new species of *Eucryphia* has been discovered on Mount Bellenden Ker in Queensland. As its leaves are pinnate it would seem to be most closely related to *E. moorei*, the other mainland species. From the look of the young plant I have recently obtained it should make a lovely small tree and it has managed to go through one Mount Macedon winter (a fairly cold one) unscathed by frost or snow.

The name for this new species has just been announced by the authorities and it is *E. wilkiei*.

P.P.S. Will wonders never cease – just as I find out the name of *E. wilkiei* I am told of another brand-new species, also from Queensland, which I haven't seen as yet. It was first found in 1994, and has just been given the name of *E. jinksii*. Could South America have yet more species awaiting discovery? It seems possible.

Euonymus alatus

Brilliantly coloured autumn foliage is not just a part of that season's glory and a useful indicator that it is in fact autumn for those of us that regularly seem to get four seasons in one day. It is also the swan song of the gardening year, a cheery finale that precedes the cold of winter and the subtle effects of deciduous trees and the fewer brave winter blooms.

Admittedly in our comparatively mild climate the garden never seems to be as fully asleep as it tends to be in far northern climates, but I feel that it is all the more important to structure our gardens to reflect the time of the year.

A garden full of evergreens will of course always look well-clothed but will lack the drama of bare stems erupting with leaves of tender green in spring, the wonderful colours of autumn foliage and the pleasing skeletons of trees and shrubs in winter. All this adds up to my main objection to a garden entirely planted with Australian native plants. About the only natives I know of that shed properly in winter are *Melia azedarach* (which isn't native only to Australia and is not renowned for its autumn colour) and *Nothofagus gunnii* from Tasmania, where it is known as 'tanglefoot' due to its twisted gnarled stems that are ready to trip the inattentive. It does colour well in autumn but it is an almost impossible challenge to those not living in cool moist hill country.

Have you noticed (getting back on track) that most of our best autumn swans tend to sing in the branches of large trees? We are all familiar with the delights of liquidambars, claret ashes and scarlet oaks, all hardy and beautiful autumn trees, but how many hardy and reliable shrubs up to 2 metres (6 ft) are there that will flaunt themselves in autumn glory? And what if we want more from our plant than a few weeks of splendour once a year?

Well here I come to the rescue again, with *Euonymus alatus*, the Winged Spindle Tree, from China and Japan.

This is but one of a huge genus of deciduous and evergreen shrubs, small trees and semi-climbing plants. There about one hundred and seventy species extending through Europe, Asia, North and Central America and Madagascar to one species in Australia.

Our selection makes a charming shrub to about 2 metres (6 ft) tall with flat fan-shaped branches. It is hardy and quick growing, not being fussy about soils and aspects.

Its tiny green flowers are of no consequence and although its berries aren't as spectacular as others in the genus they are none the less a feature. The fruit is a usually four-lobed affair, of a dark reddish colour, that splits along the seams to expose bright orange seeds.

In the autumn leaf department it turns a brilliant and unusual shade of cerise pink. Try planting clumps of bright pink nerines at its feet for a dramatic effect.

This isn't the end of the story, because its layered branches are covered in wings of corky bark that make a most interesting tracery throughout the winter. Those with a bent towards floral art will immediately see the possibilities that these fascinating winged branches have, especially those drawn toward the modern oriental styles. You know the sort of thing I mean: one twig, a flower and some rocks, classic Japanese understatement.

There seems to be much confusion over the derivation of the name *Euonymus*, one reference told me that it was just the ancient Greek name, another suggested that it comes from a Greek word, *euonumus*, meaning 'well named', and yet another said it was from a word denoting pregnancy! Perhaps I may

ıggest this last was due to the swollen berries.
By the way, the common name of spindle ·ee is usually applied to another species called . *europaeus* and not because it's spindly but because its hard wood was used to make spindles for spinning wheels. So our well-named pregnant lady could make her own baby clothes!

Euphorbia mellifera

The only continent on earth that doesn't have a species of the giant genus *Euphorbia* is probably Antarctica. This highly successful group has been able to find niches in most climates from the tropics to arid deserts, to the mountains and cool woodlands.

Although some of its species have brilliant red or orange flowers this genus has made green-coloured flowers something of a speciality. Before some pedantic reader beats me to the punch, I should point out that the flowers are usually quite small and that the green colour of the flower heads is due to green leafy bracts. As these bracts are much firmer than the petals of most other plants the show can last for a considerable time. Those that have a passion for flower arrangement will appreciate the lovely heads of green. They have probably already discovered that plants in this genus have sticky white latex-type sap that is messy to work with and usually poisonous. So take my advise and don't eat it or get it into your eyes or open wounds. The active principles comprise co-carcinogenic diterpene esters. The effects may vary depending on the season or stage of growth but they remain toxic even with dried material.

None of the above scary information need worry you unduly and it hasn't stopped me from growing, picking and enjoying plants in this useful group.

The name *Euphorbia* commemorates Euphorbius, physician to King Juba II of Mauritania in the first century AD, who used the latex for medical purposes. Many people still recommend it as a wart killer, although I have no idea if Euphorbius used it in this way.

From this genus of some two thousand species I have selected a rare shrubby species from Madeira, called *Euphorbia mellifera*. It is rare both in the wild and unfortunately in cultivation and I hope by the end of this effusion you may think it worth your while to obtain one.

It is one of the few cold-hardy shrubby species of its genus and requires nothing more than a well-drained soil and an open sunny aspect.

Allow it room to show itself off as it will make a plant about 2.5 metres (8 ft) each way in as little as three or four years; it will then slow down and thicken up. Its eventual size is usually about 3 metres (10 ft) each way.

Its rather even domed shape is just one of its claims to fame. The foliage is impressive, being a rich mid green, sessile and narrow, and if it did no more it would still be worth obtaining.

In spring for about two months it will produce large heads of honey-scented green-bracted flowers tinged with bronze. These are followed by bright green seed capsules, which have interesting ribs and bumps over their surfaces somewhat like strange hieroglyphics.

If you wish to have more *E. mellifera*, collect the seeds before they have a chance to explode from the pods or keep an eagle eye out for self-sown seedlings, which are always a possibility. These should be lifted whilst small as they don't shift well later on.

Because it is a comparatively bulky shrub you may well wish to have only one, but even in a smallish garden space must be found for this extremely handsome shrub.

Pruning is to be avoided as it is only likely to ruin the symmetry of your specimen. It would be far better to plant it well into the border so that it doesn't swamp the path and to move other plants away from it as it fills out.

For a plant that comes from dry rocky soil along the coast of its native country it is a surprisingly lush and attractive shrub that shouldn't be difficult in most antipodean gardens.

By the way, *mellifera* appropriately means 'honey-scented'.

Exochorda giraldii

It always amazes me that the small genus *Exochorda* (Pearl Bush) has only recently started to regain popularity. Fifteen years ago I was told about these plants and started to propagate them, but to my dismay no-one would buy my stock. I suppose at that time I was ahead of the trend, as everyone was planting native Autralian plants and deciduous shrubs were anathema to most gardeners. Yet one could still sell forsythias and weigelas.

Pearl bushes are just as easy to propagate and to grow on as these others and I think even more beautiful. At least in Victoria they have at last come into prominence due to the opening of the garden at Bolobek, probably one of our grandest thanks to Lady Law Smith's faultless eye for design and her wide-ranging knowledge and appreciation of plants. Anyone who has seen the two large specimens there, one on each side of a path, has quickly retreated to their cars and rushed up to see me to get a pearl bush of their own.

The two species most likely to be met with in Australia are *Exochorda giraldii* and *E. racemosa*. Both are beautiful large shrubs and very similar, so it doesn't matter too much which you get. The first one has slightly larger flowers and the second has a more spreading habit. Both are hardy and grow to about 4 metres (13 ft). They will grow in any reasonable soil in a sunny aspect or even in part shade. No regular pruning is required, although an odd thinning of older wood won't hurt.

The only drawback when growing *Exochorda* is that it is definitely a plant for one season only, as its leaves are at best ordinary and only turn a light yellow in autumn. If this worries you why not try planting a herbaceous climber at its feet which can clamber up and over it during summer and so extend the season of colour. Two suggestions would be the perennial sweet pea (*Lathyrus latifolia*) in either its white or pink form, or *Tropaeolum tuberosum*, which produces lovely orange and yellow flowers in autumn.

Getting back to the pearl bush, its common name has arisen due to the flower buds, which have a passing resemblance to a string of pearls. These little white orbs open to become virtually flat clear white blooms with a green centre. In fact a more pure white flower would be hard to find.

If the size of *E. giraldii* worries you then perhaps you might like to try *E.* × *macrantha* 'The Bride', with its relaxed arching to weeping habit at about half the height. It has only just become available in Australia, though it came into cultivation in England in 1938. Since then it has received an Award of Merit in 1973, an Award of Garden Merit in 1984 and a First Class Certificate in 1985. *E. giraldii* has, I think unfairly, missed out on any awards.

Like so many other good garden plants, *E. giraldii* is native to China, extending into Turkestan. The genus, which consists of four or five species, belongs to that indispensable family Rosaceae.

I cannot finish this profile without mentioning that *Exochorda* also makes a good cut flower as it lasts well in a vase and doesn't really need the help of other blooms to make a statement.

Fagus sylvatica 'Pendula'

It is self-evident, by the number of weeping cherries, birches, elms and others that can be seen gracing gardens everywhere, that people love weeping trees. They are lovely when well placed as accent trees, but has it ever dawned on you how formal they tend to look? If formality is your intention, then plant away.

However, there are many trees that have pendulous branches but don't look like vegetable umbrellas with straight trunks and drooping branches shooting out from one point. These trees can give a graceful and informal look to a garden. They are normally grafted low to the ground and have upward-growing leaders whilst the laterals sweep towards the ground. Certainly they will grow a good deal taller than conventional weepers, but after all the spread of a tree is often more important than its height.

I would much prefer to plant, say, *Betula pendula* 'Tristis', with its narrow habit and drooping limbs, than *B. pendula* 'Youngii', which looks like a mushroom and tends to poke you in the eye as you pass.

Another tree that has this natural weeping form is *Fagus sylvatica* 'Pendula', the Weeping Beech. An aged specimen can be truly awe-inspiring, as I hope the accompanying picture will show. This particular specimen is growing at the famous Alton garden at Mount Macedon (unfortunately not often open to the public) and has been classified by the National Trust of Australia (Victoria) in its Register of Significant Trees of Victoria.

If your garden is not of the same scale as Alton don't be put off, it has taken more than one human lifetime to reach its present size.

In spring the foliage is a most beautiful pale lime-green that darkens only slightly during summer, and then turns a deep coppery brown before falling. So although it doesn't produce showy flowers like a cherry (which only last for a week anyway) it does make a lovely year-round tree.

It is not a difficult tree to grow, but does prefer a sheltered garden and always does best in deep moisture-retentive soils.

Fothergilla major

Fothergilla major is one of North America's most beautiful autumn-colouring shrubs. I make no apologies for writing about a plant for cool mountainous climates, after all that is where I garden and some of you may well be in the same lucky state. Those who aren't may be green with envy after reading the following, but I will still read about tropical plants I can't grow and wistfully wish I could for a few seconds and then feel somewhat smug that I can grow *Fothergilla*.

So read on regardless and at the end console yourselves with the thought that I can't grow bougainvillea and would love to, whilst yours is looking a picture.

If like me you can grow it make sure you do. Its autumn foliage is stunning. If grown in heavy shade, which is probably the only spot for it away from the hills, it will turn rich bright yellow. Planted where it gets sunlight, making sure that the roots are well mulched, it will go yellow in the centre of the bush with shades of orange, scarlet and burgundy towards the outside.

As the plant rarely exceeds 1.5 metres (5 ft) tall and about the same in width you will have colour from ground level up to eye level instead of well above you, as most autumn colours tend to be.

This plant does more than just colour in autumn so it more than pays for its space. In late winter and early spring, before its leaves get under way, the bare branches are generously scattered with fluffy, slightly scented, creamy-white flowers, not unlike those of some of our native melaleucas.

For those who can grow it, you may like to know that more can be propagated from layers or rooted suckers. This way you needn't stop at one and if you feel generous you may even share some with deserving friends.

If you find a plant labelled as *F. monticola* you haven't found another species, just another *F. major*. *F. gardenii* is, however, different; it colours equally well in autumn, has slightly smaller leaves and doesn't grow quite as tall. All in all, it isn't that much different although it is in no way inferior.

In case you were thinking that if you can't have *F. major* you could try *F. gardenii*, I must point out that it isn't any hardier.

The generic name always, for me at least, brings to mind prehistoric creatures or reptiles like Gila monsters. Just as well the true owner of the name that is commemorated with this shrub isn't around to hear me say this. He was Dr John Fothergill (1712-1780), a Quaker physician from Essex who in his spare time collected and grew North American plants.

I must assume that this genus was named after him on his deathbed or just after the funeral, as it is was introduced in 1780.

Since that time it has regularly come to the attention of the Royal Horticultural Society, who bestowed several accolades. It was given two Awards of Merit, one in 1927 and one in 1937. It then obtained two First Class Certificates, one in 1969 and one (as *F. monticola*) in 1971 and the top Award of Garden Merit in 1984. Those of you who can't grow it must by now realise what you are missing out on.

If you do have a rich acid soil that doesn't dry out and in which you can grow rhododendrons, give it a try. Similarly it should grow where its relatives the witch-hazels (*Hamamelis*) flourish.

Now that we have gone through all of the above and you have convinced yourself that it may grow for you, how will we use it in the garden?

Isolated splendour is definitely one option. It could be used amongst rhododendrons to add

autumn interest, or you could try a combination that I find pleasing. Plant a cluster of *Fothergilla* next to a drift of *Hydrangea quercifolia*, preferably in the double-flowered form called 'Snowflake' if you can get it. This hydrangea has stunning foliage and will give wonderful burgundy colour in autumn to complement the *Fothergilla* and carry on through winter when its companion is bare. It will produce its large white panicles throughout summer when *Fothergilla* is just greenery. Underplant with the lovely white-leafed *Lamium* 'White Nancy' and you will have a stunning planting to be copied.

Franklinia alatamaha

Some rare plants are so beautiful, easy to propagate and undemanding in their requirements you have to wonder why they are rare at all. Of course this depends to an extent on your definition of rare.

There are plants that are rare in the wild as opposed to those that are rare in cultivation. It is sometimes quite risky to use the term at all, although it is a very handy one for nurserymen like me as it adds a certain status that customers often find irresistible.

When you actually aquire a plant that has been extinct in the wild since 1790 just think how much awe you will inspire. This is nearly as good as having a pet dodo.

The plant in question was native to a very small area of two or three acres in Georgia, USA. It was called *Franklinia alatamaha* by John Bartram, who discovered it in 1765. The genus commemorates that famous statesman, scientist and philosopher Benjamin Franklin and the strange species name is from the Altamaha river, which flows through the original habitat.

Those of an observant disposition may have noticed that the species name has one more 'a' than the river and some authorities do cut out the extra one. Bartram described it as 'a flowering tree of the first order of beauty and fragrance of blossoms'. His son William introduced it to cultivation when he collected seed on one of his expeditions in the 1770s. Some of the seeds were grown in the Bartram garden in Philadelphia, one of which survived into the twentieth century. All the plants now grown are believed to have originated from this source.

The last wild plants may well have become extinct due to natural causes such as flooding, although the Audubon Society's *Field Guide to American Trees* also suggests that it may have been collected wholesale for shipment to London nurseries. This seems unlikely, as mature specimens would hardly have been easy to handle and ship at 20 metres (65 ft) tall. It is by the way usually only 5 to 7 metres (16 ft 6in to 23 ft) in cultivation.

In the United States the franklinia is grown as far north as Boston and it also survives Ohio's freezing winters. It is hardest to grow in its native South as it is susceptible to a root rot spread by cotton. Some botanists have suggested that this may be why it died out in Georgia.

Franklinia is a member of the Camellia family, Theaceae, and is most closely allied to the better known *Gordonia*. *The New Royal Horticultural Society Dictionary of Gardening* has actually sunk the *Gordonia* genus into *Franklinia*, which changes the previously monotypic *Franklinia* genus into one that now has some seventy species. Other authorities who won't leave it by itself tend to make *Franklinia* part of *Gordonia*.

Franklinia does however differ from *Gordonia* because of its deciduous habit, its almost sessile flowers and the curious zigzag dehiscense of the seed capsule. Just to confuse the issue even further, a hybrid with *Gordonia lasianthus* (the loblolly bay) was produced in America in 1977, so this may or may not be an intergenetic hybrid.

Apart from an interesting history what does *Franklinia* have to offer us gardeners?

It is a small deciduous tree with handsome fragrant pure white flowers that perform in late summer and autumn, a particularly useful time to have dramatic flowers on trees as few seem to do their thing then. These single camellia-like blooms are usually about 8 cm (3 in) across and liberally produced on a well-established plant.

This is definitely not a one-act performance as its foliage will usually start to colour well before the flowering season is over. It is a truly arresting if slightly odd sight to see a plant with

nasses of scarlet, orange and yellow leaves berally studded with large white flowers.

Another attractive feature is the shape of the ree. It has a fairly narrow upright habit that von't take up much room and the branches re arranged in tiers so that even when naked n the winter it makes an interesting silhouette.

Although it will tolerate a slightly alkaline soil should have ample organic material. Plant it in sheltered aspect with morning sun and all hould be well. If you are already growing amellias then similar conditions will suit. I do in fact regularly recommend a franklinia as a good companion for rhododendrons, camellias and azaleas as it gives colour in late summer and autumn to liven up their dark green foliage and its shape is a pleasing contrast to their more compact outline.

The reason it is rarely written about is that most of our gardening books originate in Britain, where the franklinia rarely thrives. This is because although it prefers a sheltered aspect it likes a more Mediterranean climate with warmer summers and cool winters.

Fremontodendron californicum

Have you been looking for a quick-flowering evergreen shrub for a hot suntrap against a wall? You want something that will be reasonably upright or could even be espaliered. It needs to have attractive foliage and showy flowers over as long a period as possible. Due to its proximity to the house the soil will be somewhat dry and it may be rather poor.

Let's make it even harder and suggest that our selection not be too dense or bushy as we wish to soften the walls without obliterating them altogether. We must have something with a perfectly safe root system as our other half is more interested in protecting the nest than in making it look good and we want a plant that isn't dead common. After all it's a prominent spot and it would be nice to wax lyrical about it when we have visitors unfamiliar with the plant.

It must be fast growing and flower young, we can't wait forever to get the effect, and finally we often get hard frosts so it must be nearly as frost-tolerant as it is heat-proof.

One would assume that if such a plant exists it could hardly stay rare for long. The nursery industry must propagate it up to such large quantities that we would be as sick of it as I'm sure you are of golden diosmas and *Pittosporum* 'James Stirling'.

Such a fabulous plant not only exists but surprise, surprise it is also available (if rarely) to Australian gardeners.

Fremontodendron californicum is a plant that will admirably fit all the above specifications.

It was discovered by and named in honour of Major-General John Charles Frémont (1813-1890). He made several very risky journeys of exploration into the far west of the United States between 1842 and 1848 and whilst dodging Indians discovered and returned with many fine plants that now grace our gardens.

It was originally named *Fremontia* by the botanist John Torrey, although the name had previously been used for quite a different plant in the Chenopodiaceae (Saltbush) family. That plant had been re-classified and placed in the genus *Sarcobatus*. Torrey thought that he was at liberty to re-use the name, but this was not so.To conform with botanical rules the name of our plant had to be changed to *Fremontodendron* (literally, Fremont tree), which still commemorates Frémont. How fortunate he was to have such a beauty named after him.

There are supposed to be two species with attendant subspecies and hybrids but it would seem that only *F. californicum* is available in Australia. This species was first introduced into England in 1851 and quite soon after, in 1866, received a First Class Certificate.

I had now better get down to the nitty-gritty and give you the good and the bad with respect to this plant. It is a quick-growing evergreen of hardy constitution, as my preamble would suggest, that usually grows to about 4 or 5 metres (13 ft to 16 ft 6 in), although it is recorded up to 10 metres (33 ft) in the wild.

It has attractive three-lobed leaves and large yellow flowers to 5 cm (2 in) across. These blooms are usually stained with deep orange on their backs and are produced in flushes throughout the warmer months, although my own tree seems never to be without some flowers even in the depths of winter.

The common name usually applied to this plant is Flannel Bush, although it is sometimes called Tree Poppy here in Australia. This isn't a good common name as it isn't a poppy and it also becomes confused with plants such as *Romneya* and *Dendromecon*, both of which deserve the common name much more.

It is called flannel bush due to the bronze bristles most prominent on the stems, flower

›uds and seed capsules as well as the back of
eaves. Flannel it might look like, but if you
ısed a face washer that irritated like asbestos
›r fibreglass fibres you would probably enjoy
ıair shirts and woollen underpants.

This and the fact that *Fremontodendron* can
›e somewhat short-lived are the only
ıegatives it has, unless of course you hate
ellow flowers. If you wear gloves and goggles
vhen you intend a major pruning you
houldn't suffer any problems and if it is
›lanted in rather poorer soils it tends to live longer, perhaps up to twenty-five years. This isn't too bad when you divide your original investment by the number of years you could have the plant.

I find that most are lost due to excessive dampness and strong winds that wrench the roots. They hate root disturbance so should be planted young, staked well and sheltered from excessive wind.

They aren't even that difficult to raise from their shiny black seeds, so there isn't any real excuse for not planting one.

Garrya flavescens

It would seem to me that there are two major kinds of gardening books. First, there are those that set out the facts about a plant like how tall it grows, where to grow it, when it flowers and so on. These works are undoubtedly of great merit. It is after all this very information that we require if we wish to grow some unknown acquisition in our gardens. Huge encyclopaedic works like the recent four-volume *New Royal Horticultural Society Dictionary of Gardening* are cases in point. One can look up a vast amount of information on how to grow literally thousands of plants.

All very good stuff I'm sure but would you sit and read it like a novel! No longer do they include information (opinionated as it would have to be) on what are the best varieties. In the previous four-volume edition one would find little asterisks beside the plant considered the best for one reason or another. I often used these little symbols if I was ordering seed of some unknown plant hoping I would get the superior forms.

This leads us to the second type of gardening book, written by authors not frightened to express their tastes. These opinionated works will often (although not always) give you the how-to-grow information as well as the important aspects of how to use them well and what makes these plants, for the authors, special.

Good writers in this genre will encourage you to read their books more like a novel. You will be able to nod sagely when you agree with them, laugh at their little asides or hotly dispute their beliefs if they don't coincide with your own. These books often assume a goodly amount of knowledge already in your possession but even a complete novice should find them stimulating. As long as you then go on to form your own opinions, they will have performed the important function of stimulating interest.

Great writers such as Reginald Farrer, who lived from 1880 to 1920, still stimulate, charm and annoy readers to this very day. His style was extremely opinionated and his disposition so argumentative that it is almost a sporting-type hobby to disagree with him and get away with it.

I would certainly not put myself in the same league as Reginald Farrer (who would dare?) but I can be as opinionated as anyone and it is about a plant that is generally dismissed, if it is mentioned at all, that I in my usual roundabout way wish to discuss.

Mention *Garrya* and it is generally agreed that only one species is of garden merit. This is of course *G. elliptica*, the Silk Tassel Tree. For those who don't know, it is a large evergreen shrub with somewhat sombre green leaves and elegant drooping catkins of a subtle grey-green colour with soft primrose stamens. These are produced in winter, when they are most useful, and although I ignore my plant most of the year I enjoy its strange effect when it is in bloom. Naturally my plant is of a superior clone, *G. elliptica* 'James Roof', whose catkins can be up to 20 cm (8 in) long, and provided the wind does not tie them in knots they are quite impressive.

Of the other species, some eighteen in number, little is written and as most have quite short catkins I can accept the far from glowing descriptions in books. So it was with some lack of enthusiasm that I propagated cuttings of *G. flavescens*, obtained (with permission) from the Royal Botanic Gardens, Melbourne.

Its foliage was far better than *G. elliptica*, being a lovely soft grey all over. Research would suggest that my plant is possibly *G. flavescens* 'Pallida', as *G. flavescens* is silver on the back of the leaf only.

When I found some references to *G. flavescens* in my library they invariably said

hat its catkins were only 3 cm long. Imagine ny surprise when it flowered and I found that t least in my plant these catkins were 15 cm 6 in) or so. Not quite up to the 'James Roof' tandards but a respectable length none the ess. I can find no mention of longer catkins vith 'Pallida'.

So why do the books all say *G. flavescens* has niserable catkins? Was I lucky that the Botanic Gardens had a superior form, or has one reference work got it wrong and the rest ollowed suit? Perhaps in England, where my books came from, it doesn't do well and is pining for its native haunts in Nevada, California and New Mexico.

Whatever the reason, I think I'm onto a good thing and I look forward to my plant reaching its full height of 3 metres (10 ft) each way. Let's hope they haven't got that wrong as well.

Finally I should mention that garryas are hardy shrubs, tolerant of pollution and maritime exposure, happy in sun or semi-shade. They can be trained as espaliers or standards if you like that sort of thing. I know I do.

Genista hispanica

You may well have noticed that I often bemoan the fact that gardeners seem to fill their gardens with lots of dense bushy plants. Bushiness seems to be the number one requirement next to indestructibility. In garden design, contrast in shape and outline is just as important as contrast in colour and texture of foliage and flowers.

Many a loosely framed plant can screen an unwanted view or give you privacy without enclosing you in a vegetable prison.

Now from the above you may think I have no use or liking for dense-growing plants and of course this isn't the case. It is more a matter of how you use them.

I love well-tended purposeful hedges that make solid architectural statements in the garden. I also get a secret kick out of well-placed and fun topiary, which can add so much whimsy at a fraction of the cost of a sculpture. Naturally bushy or even formal-shaped plants can be used to frame a view, define an end or give structure to a host of fluffy perennials or formless roses.

I think I have just offended a whole new section of my readership! Assuming of course that you are still with me.

Another effect that can be most attractive is the tight undulating look obtained when several plants of the one variety with a tight domed shape are planted together. You can make your own miniature cluster of hills and if you think yourself small much harmless pleasure can be had strolling over them in your mind's eye.

This effect can easily be overdone so some restraint is required; just consider those gardens planted by lovers of heathers and dwarf ericas and you will probably know what I mean.

Now that I have managed to offend yet another special-interest gardening group I had better move on to the plant that I like making mini hills and valleys with, known botanically as *Genista hispanica*.

Genista is one of the genera in the Pea family (Leguminosae) that are often known as broom, although my selection is usually called Spanish Gorse.

As the common name would suggest, it is a native of Spain but also can be found in the south of France. What a hard life it must lead!

For most of the year it is a deep green hummock of spiny branches, usually no more than 70 cm (2 ft 3 in) tall but with age it may cover 2 metres (6 ft) or more of ground. Quite obviously vast numbers are usually unnecessary, especially if your garden isn't large. Most people don't notice that this plant is actually deciduous and holds leaves for only a short time each year, the job of photosynthesis being done by its green stems.

For several weeks in late spring your hummocks of green will literally turn brilliant golden yellow with hardly a bit of green showing. To see it in masses on the dry stony hills of France and Spain must surely be a sight to create sore eyes.

If my idea of hills doesn't appeal, use just one plant and mix it with other things that revel in the heat in well-drained poorish soils. Cistus, lavenders and rosemary are suitable companions, or even some of our own dry-country natives, as long as you are not a purist.

Once it is installed in a suitable environment then you can sit back and enjoy the show. Its tight groundcovering habit will swamp all but the most pernicious weeds, which is just as well as its a real pain to weed anything out of it. A light trimming over after flowering can be done if you feel the need, although I find it rarely necessary unless my valleys need redefining. Don't cut it back into old brown wood as it isn't likely to reshoot well.

Young pot-grown plants will settle in uickly and within a year or so be giving of ıeir best. Don't ever try to shift it as it rarely ·ansplants well, like so many other plants in ıe Pea family.

Genista is a name used by Virgil, which may or may not have originally been used for this genus of plants (probably not). It is also where the Plantagenet Kings and Queens of England derived their name (Planta genista). Their choice would seem appropriate as they were every bit as prickly as *Genista hispanica*.

Ginkgo biloba 'Fastigiata'

Trees or shrubs with a pencil-shaped habit usually don't look natural. Somehow poplars and pencil pines manage at least to look as if they should be that shape but many other fastigiate varieties of normal-shaped (whatever that means) trees can look quite artificial or even odd. I might add that I think it is harder to over-use fastigiate plants than standard grafted weeping trees, which look completely contrived and rather formal and somehow even slightly smug.

Now don't get me wrong, I have nothing against a touch, or even a lot, of formality in gardens. They are after all the creations of man not of nature and plants with a formal shape can make great garden ornaments. A pencil pine is a good alternative to an obelisk and is usually easier to install and far cheaper. A weeping birch may well make an inexpensive alternative to a fountain and anything clipped to shape can be used as a living statue.

Sticking with the fastigiates (I hope everyone has by now realised that this means 'pencil shaped'), these tall slender plants can have many practical and aesthetic applications in the garden apart from obelisk impersonation.They make good feature trees or exclamations in the landscape that will draw the eye in their direction and maybe away from the clothes line. As formal pairs on either side of a path they will frame the view or lead you in the right direction. Whilst on pairs I might add that it is an unwritten law (until now) that one tree must grow faster than the other or die just as they have grown too tall to buy a similar sized replacement.

They can be very useful in those silly narrow beds that driveway makers insist on leaving between their handiwork and the boundary. They will then give height and some screening without scratching the car or imposing on your neighbour's air space.

It always amazes me how many quite unrelated plants have produced fastigiate forms. Apart from the many conifers and poplars one can obtain svelte forms of oak, hornbeam, birch, beech, tulip tree, cherry, crabapple, maple and even a ginkgo.

As everyone knows, the ginkgo is the last surviving member of a once widespread group of conifers related to (but not resembling) plants that would have been in a dinosaur's diet. Fossil remains of *Ginkgo* have been found around the world and are dated back at least 180 million years. It has survived in only China and Japan and is usually found as a cultivated tree near Buddhist temples. Frank Meyer, the Dutch-American plant collector, is believed to have seen *G. biloba* growing in the wild, west of Hang-chow, possibly in 1906. There is some evidence to suggest that truly wild plants still exist in remote mountain areas in Chekiang and Anhwei Provinces. It could be argued that planting them in Australia is only reintroducing a native plant.

The common name of Maidenhair Tree alludes to the leaf shape being similar to the pinnules of the maidenhair fern (*Adiantum*). The botanical name derives from the Japanese rendering of one of its Chinese names, Yin-kuo, which means 'silver apricot'. This in turn alludes to the kernels of the seed which are much prized and said to be an aid to digestion and to diminish the effects of drinking.

I might add that the pulp on the outside of the seed stinks as it rots and it is best to obtain a male tree if you can, to avoid seed production. This fastigiate form is male so this is another good reason to plant it.

Sir James Smith tried to have the name *Ginkgo* dropped as he considered it quite uncouth and replaced with *Salisburia*. I hope someone of the day pointed out that his surname was also a bit on the common side and he should become Sir James Salisburia instead.

In Australia the oldest and biggest ginkgo is growing in the Botanic Gardens at Geelong, Victoria. This most impressive specimen was planted in 1859 and is producing strange aerial-root-like growths from the trunk that look like melted wax. This characteristic would seem to be uncommon and isn't often mentioned in books. Some trees in China are supposed to be over a thousand years old.

If you visit the big specimens to be seen in many public gardens you may well be pleased you selected *G. biloba* 'Fastigiata' instead of the usual spreading form. It will certainly be more manageable in gardens and each autumn you will have a pillar of gold before the leaves shed.

Ginkgo in any of its forms is usually a fairly hardy if slow-growing tree, not fussy about soil types and usually immune to diseases, pests and pollution.

So next time you are looking for trees don't dismiss the weight watchers' dinosaur dinner, *Ginkgo biloba* 'Fastigiata'. My eight-year-old plant is about 3.5 metres (12 ft) tall and only a slender 1 metre (3 ft) wide.

Glyptostrobus pensilis

People tend to fall into one of two camps when it comes to conifers: those who love them and those who don't. The affirmatives can be further subdivided into smaller more specialist groups. There are the lovers of all things small, with gardens full of rocks and alpine plants. They see dwarf conifers as essential backbone plants and may even use effusive adjectives like 'cute' and 'sweet' when describing their favourites.

Other people love the sombre grandeur of towering spruces, pines and cedars and if their gardens aren't large they probably live in eternal gloom.

Finally there are the neat brigade, who like blue spruces and narrow junipers because they always look tidy and don't make a mess in the swimming pool.

Those who dislike this group of plants probably also fit into a particular niche.

There are the ill-informed lot who have yet to see them used well. Conifers for them bring forth visions of golden book-leafed thujas alternated with standard roses (various colours) lining concrete paths. Or perhaps they have seen the gardens of the towering-tree lovers and feel that they would like to have some lawn left.

Another group consists of what I would call the trendy fraternity, who look down their respective noses at all conifers as something vulgar and suburban, unless of course they are growing in Versailles tubs and clipped into balls on sticks.

This huge family of plants has so much diversity that it is patently obvious they can't all be dismissed or indeed embraced as good garden plants.

The conifer about which I am now going to write may well appeal to some or even all of the above groups and even to those who don't fit snugly into any.

Glyptostrobus pensilis is quite rare, so that should appeal to the snobs amongst us. It may well even be extinct in the wild in its southern China home. It did, however, have the good sense to become lucky! The Chinese regularly plant it to bring luck to the home and the rice crop. One might say it is a case of being lucky to be lucky, unlike a rabbit's foot!

For those who think of conifers as dark and gloomy, *Glyptostrobus* usually comes as something of a surprise. Its foliage is a light grey-green through spring and summer, then in autumn and early winter it turns a lovely coppery pink and slowly sheds. Deciduous conifers are few and far apart, so don't tend to make the press with Australian horticulturists.

When it does turn colour it holds it for ages and to see it glowing in the low rays of the early winter sun can be most rewarding. I have, however, had people ask me why I haven't pulled out that dead tree. I usually don't respond to such comments.

The habit of this plant is also light and airy and yet its overall outline has that conical symmetry often expected of conifers. As the tree ages it will develop pleasant furrowed grey-brown bark.

Unlike its deciduous relatives the dawn redwood and the North American swamp cypress (*Metasequioa* and *Taxodium* respectively), this is a smallish slow-growing tree, mine is a bit over 4 metres (13 ft) after about twelve years. Although specimens of up to 25 metres (80 ft) have been recorded I expect to be long gone when mine reaches these lofty dimensions.

It is often mistaken for a *Taxodium* but is botanically different due to its pear-shaped long-stalked cones, obovate scales and small winged seeds. Visually it is, as before mentioned, a smaller tree. It is also slightly finer in foliage and better in its summer and autumn colours.

Like the *Taxodium* it is also tolerant of damp to wet sites, in fact one is supposed to be able to plant a young tree up to half its height under water in a slow-moving stream or dam. This is even more than the average *Taxodium* will tolerate. I do, however, think it would be safer to plant it at water's edge unless it needs protection from herbivores that can't swim or wade; it is also more comfortable for the planter as well as the plant.

Although the Chinese Swamp Cypress (as *Glyptostrobus* is sometimes called) isn't considered hardy in England few areas in Australia would have a cold enough climate to affect it, so as long as the soil stays moist to wet it could well be worthwhile trying.

By the way, its strange botanical name comes from the Greek *glypto*, which means 'to carve', and *strobilos*, which means 'cone'. This is an allusion to the depressions on the cone scales. The species name *pensilis* means 'hanging down', which also alludes to the cones.

You may also see this tree listed as *G. lineatus*, which is a name that most authorities expect should sink into synonymy. I just hope you don't sink into obscurity whilst planting your *Glyptostrobus*.

Hypericum 'Rowallane'

The genus *Hypericum* is a large one of some four hundred species, almost cosmopolitan in its distribution although it is rarely represented in tropical lowlands, the Arctic (and one must assume the Antarctic), really high altitudes or desert regions.

Due to its dispersion it contains plants of various types from low herbaceous plants and groundcovers to large shrubs; some are even aquatic.

Having said this, it is surprising that the flower shape (not size) is remarkably uniform and that this genus makes a speciality of the colour yellow. I have yet to meet an hypericum in flower that looks like anything other than an hypericum.

William T. Stearn's *Dictionary of Plant Names for Gardeners* tells us that the botanical name comes from the Greek word *hypereikon* and is supposed to be from either *ereike*, 'a heath' (I can't see the connection) or *hyper*, which means 'above',and *eikon*, 'a picture'.

The plant was supposed to keep away evil spirits and the flowers were once placed above pictures to ward off evil at the ancient midsummer festival Walpurgisnacht. This pagan rite was later swallowed up by Christendom as the Feast Day of St John (24 June). The common name of the genus thus became St John's Wort. Wort means 'plant' and has nothing to do with warts, which is how many people pronounce the word. I am somewhat relieved that it isn't known as Walpurgisnacht's Wort.

If you look closely at the leaf of an hypericum you may be able to detect tiny transparent glands. To revenge himself on the plant the devil apparently pierced the leaf with a needle. This would seem to have been a pretty childish prank for such a powerful being, if you ask me.

It is amongst the shrubby hypericums that you will find some of the best garden plants and amongst these you may like to try one of my favourites, *Hypericum* 'Rowallane'.

This lovely flowering shrub was discovered as a chance seedling at Rowallane, Hugh Armytage-Moore's garden in Northern Ireland. Now a National Trust garden, Rowallane has also given us new varieties of *Chaenomeles*, *Primula* and *Viburnum*.

Our hypericum is most likely a cross between *H. leschenaultii* and *H. hookerianum* 'Charles Rogers'.

It makes an attractive more or less evergreen shrub with upright canes and arching branches up to about 3 metres (10 ft) tall and not much more than 1 metre (3 ft) in width, making it ideal in narrow beds or as a feature plant to add height to an otherwise low planting of other shrubs or perennials.

The large saucer-shaped rich yellow flowers can be up to 7.5 cm (3 in) across and contain a boss of attractive stamens. The flowering season is an extensive one, usually throughout summer and autumn although I often have blooms well into winter. It is definitely not a one week wonder.

It will grow quickly in any average soil and although it blooms more prolifically in a sunny aspect it will still perform quite well in semi-shade. You can also expect flowers in the first year from cuttings so you needn't have much patience. By the way it is also quite easy to propagate from semi-hardwood or hardwood pieces.

Pruning is usually done, if needed, in late winter or early spring and consists of the complete removal of the oldest spent canes. This will invigorate the plant, which will then send up several new watershoots from ground level. In this way you won't loose its elegant habit, as you undoubtedly would if you trimmed it.

H. 'Hidcote' received an Award of Merit in 1954 and *H.* 'Rowallane' received the same award in 1943, plus a well-deserved Award of Garden Merit in 1984.

So if you are having a devil of a time in the garden perhaps you can change your luck by planting a St John's Wort, although it is unlikely to have many blooms on his feast day down under.

Ilex verticillata

It is always fun to grow a plant from a well-known genus that isn't in what is usually considered the classic mould. Many such groups have but one or two often-cultivated species, and at least to the uninitiated unless a plant looks like the recognised types, it can't possibly be one.

Such a plant is *Ilex verticillata*, from eastern North America. It doesn't have spiny holly-like leaves and it isn't even evergreen.

Many customers ask me about the shrub with the lovely red berries and I invariably get a look of disbelief when I tell them it's a holly.

It may not look all that much like a holly, but it is a useful and attractive shrub for the garden. Plant it in a sunny but moist to wet position (it grows in swampy ground in its native home) and you will end up with a shrub of 2 or 3 metres (6 to 10 ft) in height, with attractive light green leaves that turn bright yellow in autumn. The masses of berries ripen in late summer and can remain on the plant well into winter, birds allowing. The first year mine fruited I had berries right through to spring but, alas, they have now been discovered by the rosella parrots so don't last that long any more.

The only drawback with this plant is that, like most other hollies, you need a male and a female to produce fruit at all. (I need hardly point out that it is only the female that produces the fruit.) This need not deter you even though the male plant doesn't do anything particularly exciting, because if you plant them both in the one hole with the male at the back the two plants will take up no more room than one would, and the female will disguise her rather drab partner. If you have room you may even like to give him a harem, as one male can service quite a number of productive females.

For a plant that was introduced into England in 1736 and received an Award of Merit in 1962 it is strange that you rarely see it in gardens here.

Illicium anisatum

If you can grow camellias in your garden then you should be able to grow members of the genus *Illicium*. This obscure genus in my humble opinion deserves to be better known and although I doubt that any of the species will ever oust the much loved camellia, I for one could live without one or two camellias to make room for one illicium.

It is a genus of some forty species scattered throughout eastern and south-eastern Asia, the West Indies and south-eastern United States and its most famous member is better known to cooks than to gardeners. This is *I. verum*, the fruits of which are sold as star anise and used in Asian cooking. They can also be used in potpourri and oils extracted from this plant are used medicinally as a stimulant, expectorant and carminative.

I don't, however, have *I. verum* in my collection so it is about some of the other species that I wish to write. Probably the most common species in cultivation (if common can be fairly used at all considering how rarely it is seen for sale) is *I. anisatum*, from China. Like the rest of the genus it is an evergreen shrub, which in this case will usually grow to 2 metres (6 ft) or so. It has a bushy but not overly dense habit and is usually narrower than it is tall.

The leaves are a glossy mid green in colour and have a lovely aromatic smell when crushed. This feature is usual with all the species and the name *Illicium* comes from the Latin word *illicio* meaning 'to attract'. So plant it where you can pluck a leaf as you pass by. The only thing to remember is that if you get carried away by this habit you could end up with a naked specimen.

In spring it is covered with quaint many-petalled pale lemon flowers. The petals are thick and waxy to the touch and unlike the leaves are virtually scentless. The overall effect is dainty rather than showy. If planted in a well-drained but moist soil in an aspect that gets morning sun or filtered light it should give you many years of pleasure. It should even grow in soils that are slightly alkaline as long as it has adequate humus.

This plant was introduced in 1790 and received an Award of Merit from the Royal Horticultural Society in 1930. Once you have it growing you will agree that it should be seen more often than it is, and you will probably be keen to try other species. With a little bit of effort you may be able to obtain two or three more.

I. floridanum has larger deeper green leaves and grows to about 3 metres (10 ft) tall. It has comparatively large starfish-like flowers which are a rich deep maroon-purple. I find it somewhat sinister in appearance, which doesn't mean that I don't like it, quite the contrary. This one comes from the southern United States.

The third species in my collection is *I. henryi*, from western China. This one is the slowest-growing of the species I have obtained but will eventually get up to 2 metres (6 ft). Its leaves are light green and glossy and the flowers are soft pink with a greenish centre. The petals are more rounded and overlapping than the two previously described. Make sure that you give this one a reasonably shaded spot as its leaves can bleach a sickly yellow in too much sun.

Finally, I have a species from Georgia and Florida, ominously calleed *I. parviflorum*. Ominous because if your botanical Latin is up to scratch you will know that *parviflorum* means 'small flowered'. In a genus not known for large showy blooms this is a worry. Its flowers are indeed quite small and not even produced in quantity. They are deep yellow and produced in summer and autumn instead of spring.

I still think it is worth growing unless you ave a very small garden. Its foliage is a lovely right mid green, and of the four species I grow ıis has the strongest scent when crushed.

I. parviflorum seems to be both sun and hade tolerant, and will grow equally well in ery damp soils through to dryish ones. This pecies reputedly grows to 4 or 5 metres (13 : to 16 ft 6 in) and in the only book I have ound it described it is supposed to be uckering in habit. I am still waiting for this ıixed blessing.

One day I hope to see *I. simonsii*, also from China and new to cultivation. This is a small shrub, to 2 metres (6 ft), with fragrant yellow flowers. It is one of more than sixteen hundred species of Asian plants collected in the wild and currently grown in California's new botanical garden, Quarryhill. Working in cooperation with British and Chinese horticulturists and botanists, Quarryhill has embarked on a mission to conserve the endangered flora of Asia.

Itea ilicifolia

What is a feature plant and what characteristics must a plant have to fit the bill?

Probably one of the most important aspects of such plants is shape. Our selected feature must stand out from the various blotches and splodges of foliage and branches that can make up the average garden plant. As long as the shape is different from things around, it should make an impact. It could be fastigiate (pencil-shaped), ball-shaped, arching or weeping.

Texture can set a plant apart, but the fleeting colour of flowers usually isn't enough. A potted azalea can look stunning whilst in flower but unless you have one with an arching habit of growth, like the lightly-fragrant 'Alba Magna', it adds little to the garden when it is without flowers. Colour of foliage is far more permanent, even deciduous plants can in this way give interest for at least nine months of the year.

Finally there are plants that just seem to have a certain indefinable presence that sets them apart. One might even say that they exude quality.

The question now arises as to the uses of such plants. They can make an eye-catching vegetable sculpture, taken to its extreme in topiary. They are certainly cheaper than buying a Henry Moore for the garden and can be your own original creation.

They can be used to direct the eye, thus leading you in a certain direction, like the front door, or away from some unattractive sight like the Hills hoist. Usually such plants need to be used with restraint as a garden full of features can be disorientating.

This at last leads us to our subject in this essay, a plant from western to central China, called *Itea ilicifolia*.

It is a plant that probably fits best in the quality class mentioned before. The mock spiny holly-like leaves are glossy, rich green and attractive but no colour break in the garden. Nor are its lovely honey-scented drooping green catkins, produced in summer but still presentable months later. Its arching habit, made even more pronounced whilst in flower, is graceful and definitely sets it apart.

A fully-grown plant is usually about 3 metres (10 ft) tall by about the same wide and requires no more attention than to remove some of the older spent canes. It likes a cool, moist but not wet soil in an aspect facing east or with filtered sun from larger trees.

It is the most striking member of its genus, which includes about ten other species native to Asia and North America and it is its American relative *I. virginica* that is the only other species met with here. This is a deciduous shrub about 1 metre (3 ft) high, with upright candles of white flowers and good autumn foliage, and the relationship between the two isn't all that obvious.

The name *Itea* comes from the Greek for 'willow' and I guess its catkins may have suggested this name to some foundering taxonomist. More appropriate is *ilicifolia*, which means 'holly-leafed', as long as we are all thinking of English holly and not one of its more obscure relatives.

It once belonged to the family Saxifragaceae but has more recently been put into Grossulariaceae (Gooseberry family) or even Iteaceae (Itea family). Plant families get nearly as much shaking up as the rest of the divisions, with genera being moved from one family to another or into totally new families. There is also a trend towards families with fewer members, rather like the human family in fact.

This plant was discovered by Augustine Henry some time prior to 1895; it received an Award of Merit in 1911, an Award of Garden

Merit in 1984 and a First Class Certificate in 1988. But for me it needs no more than to have seen it growing by the Lutyens circular steps in Christopher Lloyd's garden at Great Dixter. I wouldn't mind having the steps as a feature either.

Jasminum fruticans

When customers enter a nursery with a particular plant in mind, say a daphne, they usually have a preconceived idea of what they will get.

Sticking with my example of a daphne, virtually everyone means that they want *Daphne odora*, at least they do if they are Australian.

If the nursery stocks a range of different species and cultivars as I do, it is usually to no avail. What they are after is an evergreen, scented, pink- to white-flowered shrub that they are familiar and comfortable with. Not something deciduous that they have never heard of, with lavender-blue flowers and no scent, such as *D. genkwa*.

Even less likely to appeal is *D. jezoensis*, with its yellow scented blooms on a bush that is summer deciduous!

Many other genera of plants have the same problem. The general public are familiar with only one or two species and these are held up as typical for the lot. If you prove that this isn't really the case, all it tends to do is confuse and unsettle them. Many people like to think that their knowledge of plants is reasonable and don't like the feeling of bewilderment that a large array of unknown species tends to engender.

Continuing with this line of thought, if a jasmine is something you thought you might like then you will probably be expecting to buy a climbing plant with highly scented blooms. Australian gardeners will usually be thinking of *Jasminum polyanthum*.

If I offer them *J. fruticans* (and I usually don't bother) it would not meet expectations and to be fair if they want a climbing plant it wouldn't suit anyway.

On the other hand if someone wants a bushy, hardy evergreen shrub and I offer this species I usually get a negative response, after all jasmines should climb, shouldn't they?

Before pointing out the attractions of this shrub that falls between stools, it is probably worth mentioning one other problem with it from the commercial point of view. It is quite quick-growing and so needs to be turned over regularly before it starts to look a bit scruffy. Although a root-bound tatty specimen will soon be off and away again once planted, customers are excusably hesitant to buy it. It also has a somewhat rangy habit whilst young so even a healthy specimen tends not to loosen most peoples' purse strings.

On the positive side, this plant is indisputably hardy and will grow in most soil types and aspects. It is happy in sun or part shade, rocky, sandy or clay soils and will cope with aplomb (once established) with drought and frost. It is in fact probably as hardy as most other plants I have written about, if not more so.

It is easy to propagate from cuttings or layers, a boon to the thrifty gardener if not to your nursery owners. Prune it as you desire and when you feel like it. You can't hurt it. You could also train it as a wall shrub if you wished to.

Although not many people may consider it a shrub of the first rank, I hope that by the time I've finished you may consider it worthy of space.

If grown freestanding it usually gets to about 2 to 3 metres (6 to 10 ft) tall, an ideal height to screen you from prying neighbours, and will grow to about the same width. As I mentioned before you could adjust this with pruning.

The more or less evergreen foliage is a good rich glossy bright green and usually consists of three to five leaflets. Its flowers are the normal jasmine shape, bright yellow and produced throughout summer, although my plant

seems rarely to be without some to brighten up the garden. Also it has no detectable perfume.

After its flowers it produces pea-sized shiny black berries that may or may not excite the floral artists amongst us.

So although it may not be the crème de la crème of the two hundred or so species of jasmine I like it and perhaps you will think more kindly of it when next you visit my nursery and see some poor root-bound scruffy specimens.

Finally, the name *Jasminum* is the late medieval Latin version of the Persian name *Jasmin* or *Jasamin* and *fruticans* comes from the Latin *frutex*, 'a shrub'. It is native to southern Europe, northern Africa and Asia Minor and has been in cultivation at least in England since about the middle of the sixteenth century.

Jovellana violacea

If you grow fuchsias and love them, then I have a plant that enjoys similar conditions and would make a perfect companion for them.

Before we continue, I don't think I have as yet insulted the fuchsia fraternity so I will just mention that I am not fond of many, especially baskets full of big blowzy bi-colours or tall rickety standards heavy to the point of snapping. I have made room in my garden for one or two of the dainty yet hardy small-flowered species and find that quite enough for me. Nor do I have the time or inclination to feed, water, train and generally pamper such plants to bring out their flouncing best. I can, however, appreciate the dedicated growers' efforts in their gardens.

Now back to where I started. If you have a moist soil and cool aspect with either morning sun or dappled shade all day and are looking for something a bit different to mix with the fuchsias or the rhododendrons or any other group of plants that prefer such conditions, then you could do worse than planting *Jovellana violacea*.

It is a member of the Scrophulariaceae (Foxglove) family, a terrible name that arose because some *Scrophularia* have swollen roots that look like scrofulous tumours, which in more naive times was a sure indication that it would cure what it looked like.

Jovellana has no such claim and is closely related to *Calceolaria*, which have strange pouched and freckled flowers. I wonder what our ancestors would have used these for medicinally had they known them. The main difference between the two genera is that *Jovellana* hasn't a pouch and its flowers look more like little puckered mouths. It is a small genus of some six species native to South America and New Zealand, but it is only *J. violacea* from Chile that you are likely to come across. The genus was named by Ruiz and Pavon after Dr Gaspar Melchor De Jovellanos (1744-1811), who was a student and patron of Peruvian flora.

Our selection is a suckering twiggy shrub that can reach 2 metres (6 ft) although it is usually less.

Its stems, like those of fuchsias, are quite brittle so plants should be sheltered from strong winds and some care must be taken not to break the stems when weeding and fiddling with them. If you do manage to snap bits it isn't a true disaster as it will soon re-shoot. It is, however, most depressing when you end up with half the plant in your hand, especially if it is just about to flower.

The leaves are small, bright green and serrated, pleasant all year if not spectacular. A good combination is to it mix it with plants of a darker larger-leafed persuasion.

It flowers from mid spring into early summer and produces masses of clustered mid mauve mouths with a yellow internal tongue and rich purple freckles. These are best described as pretty, if you know what I mean. They have a daintiness that precludes using adjectives like 'spectacular'.

As far as regular care is concerned, all that is required is the complete removal of old spent stems every year or so. It will soon replace them with suckers.

These suckers are an easy way to propagate more plants, although it strikes quite easily from semi-hardwood cuttings as well.

Whilst on the subject of suckering, many people have a fear of such plants but in this case they needn't worry. It doesn't wander far and is most useful to fill irregular gaps between more substantial shrubs.

Young plants will start blooming from twelve months old so you will not have to wait ages for colour and if happy with your selected site should be of close to mature size in about three years.

Finally, it was introduced into cultivation in about 1853 and received an Award of Merit in 1930.

Kalmia angustifolia 'Nana'

A slightly worrying trend has come to my attention recently, and that is possible government legislation requiring nurseries to print a warning on labels and in catalogues if a plant is potentially poisonous. If the seed catalogues are any indication, it would seem that this may be the case already in England.

Don't get me wrong, I am all in favour of being well-informed, but this sort of Big Brother attitude has, I think, many drawbacks.

When I am selling a plant I usually mention any poisonous properties it may have. Apart from the hassles of writing this warning on the label as I would have to do, because most of what I grow doesn't possess a printed label, aren't I admitting liability just as the owner of a vicious dog is when he puts up a sign saying 'Beware of the Dog'. Does this liability still exist when the label disappears?

On another level, do we really have to go to these extremes to protect individuals from themselves? Children should be trained from an early age not to put things in their mouths and adults should know better. Besides, it would be interesting to know just how many people are poisoned by *Aconitum* salads or *Actaea* jam. At the risk of sounding hard and unfeeling I am tempted to suggest that it serves them right.

Another important consideration is just how deadly a plant should be before it is considered a risk. After all, many substances are dangerous if taken in large enough quantities, including the best of whiskies. There are also some nursery plants (not too many, I hope) whose foliage can be an irritant even to people without allergies. Should this be mentioned on the label?

It must also be remembered that many rare plants are an unknown quantity in this respect. So do I stop growing plants I am not sure about, just in case?

All of the above is of course to cover my rear as I launch into describing what is a potentially quite poisonous plant, assuming that you eat it.

Kalmia angustifolia 'Nana' is a dwarf form of what is usually considered to be a poor relative of the sumptuous *K. latifolia* (Mountain Laurel). I have to admit that if a direct comparison is made it does lack the dramatic impact but in its own right it is a pleasant, appealing dwarf shrub that is in fact easier to grow than its aristocratic brethren.

In its North American home it is known as 'Sheep Laurel', which conjures up images of lovely fluffy white woolly things, until you find out that it is also called by the much more direct name of 'Lamb Kill'! This last name is usually not mentioned by those wishing to sell the thing.

Ignoring its sinister side and focusing on its visual appeal, what you will end up with is a neat shrub to about 30 cm (12 in) tall with a slightly suckering habit. Its foliage is soft green although in cool to cold climates expect the leaves to droop and go bronze in winter. This characteristic isn't as unattractive as it sounds once you know it isn't dying.

It flowers in late spring and produces clusters of tiny deep pink cup-shaped flowers at the base of the last set of growth.

Like most of the rest of its family (Ericaceae) it likes a humus-rich acidic soil that never dries out and as long as it is well mulched will be happy in semi-shade or sun.

Its dwarf stature makes it a good rock-garden subject or tub specimen and it can also be used in beds that are full of rhododendrons and azaleas to add a bit of light relief.

The more usually met with taller form is also valuable if you would like a 2 metre (6 ft) shrub with an open habit (dare I call it leggy?) that can happily nestle amongst larger azaleas and rhododendrons.

Finally, this small genus of some seven pecies was named by Linnaeus after one of is pupils, Peter Kalm (1715-1779), who was ent to North America in 1748 by the wedish government to report on the ountry's natural resources. He later wrote a book on his findings and exploits.

I wonder if he was flattered having a poisonous genus named after him? I'm sure he was, since we appreciate them, as he should have, for their beauty and not for the potential to wipe out unwanted dinner guests.

Latua pubiflora

In late winter and early spring the garden is usually dominated by yellow, unless you are one of the white garden brigade who go out of their way to avoid colour.

At this time of the year we have drifts of daffodils, primroses, forsythia, kerria and acacias in every shade from palest lemon to richest gold. This is probably as it should be; after all, yellow is the colour of spring. It brightens those less than sunny days often experienced at the end of winter and makes us feel better knowing that the warmer days are (hopefully) just around the corner.

As lovely as all this is at the beginning of the gardening year, it is nice to have strongly contrasting colours to relieve the monotone of all that yellow.

I really don't like pink with my yellows, so *Prunus* and *Ribes* (flowering currant) are kept well away. I can't, however, get enough blue, mauve or purple flowering shrubs to mix with the yellows.

At ground level this isn't a problem as many early-flowered bulbs and perennials exhibit these desirable colours, but shrubs and trees in the purple to blue tones that flower in late winter and spring are less available.

If you don't like purple and yellow together perhaps you had best not read on. If you do like purple but not with yellow, you still may wish to grow the shrub I am going to suggest. Plant it somewhere else in the garden and try teaming it with something else.

The help at hand to nod its purple bells above your drifts of daffodils is called *Latua pubiflora*, from southern Chile.

It is a monotypic genus in the rather dangerous family Solanaceae, whose ninety genera and some two thousand six hundred species are distributed throughout the world, with the greatest number in South America. Many of its members are highly poisonous, though some also have medicinal uses. As well as species with edible fruit, such as capsicums and tomatoes, there are also many popular garden flowers, including salpiglossis and petunias.

Latua itself is decidedly poisonous. In fact, it contains alkaloids such as hyoscyamine and scopolamine (which aren't ingredients of breakfast cereals even if they sound as if they are!). This plant was once used by South American Indians as a malevolent hallucinogen, leading to permanent madness, and also as a fish poison. So don't be tempted to use this lovely plant as a salad garnish.

This shrub is semi-deciduous, with elegant arching canes supporting drooping swollen trumpet flowers from late winter to well into spring. They are about 4.5 cm ($1^3/4$ in) long from the calyx to the tips of the protruding stamens and are a lovely rich purple. If you look closely you will see the flowers are covered in tiny bristles, hence the species name *pubiflora*.

The one and only reference to this plant that I have found suggests that it grows to 10 metres (33 ft) in the wild but I have found in my garden that a well-grown plant is unlikely to exceed 3 metres (10 ft).

Its open elegant habit displays the flowers to perfection so you shouldn't attempt to prune it into a bushy shrub as this would defeat the purpose. If you need to screen a view, plant something bushy behind it and leave the latua alone. Perhaps something with pale green or even yellow foliage would be a suitable background.

Because of its open habit it allows ample light to grow small bulbs or perennials up to its trunk. Just watch yourself if you are planting under it or weeding around as it has got fairly well-armed branches. The spines are quite long but nowhere near as sharp as roses,

:or are they hooked so they don't stay with ou when you leap back muttering expletives.

I have found it to be hardy at Mount /lacedon to both heat and cold and although know our climate isn't extreme in either :irection I don't see any reason why most gardeners in southern Australia or New Zealand shouldn't succeed with it.

Give it a well-drained but not too dry an aspect in semi-shade or sun, then sit back and enjoy its purple trumpets for months.

Leycesteria crocothyrsos

A shrub that makes a good garden plant but will probably never be commonly available is *Leycesteria crocothyrsos*, from the mountains of Assam and northern Burma.

It isn't due to anything like difficulty of propagation, in fact it can be struck with almost embarrassing ease from semi-hardwood cuttings. Nor is it difficult to grow as it grows with remarkable speed and needs nothing more than a well-drained but not too dry an aspect in sun or semi-shade.

The reasons that you are not likely to come across this desirable shrub are mainly due to its poor performance in pots. It will grow well for a short time and then, like buddlejas, become quickly root-bound and look scruffy. So if it doesn't sell within a few weeks it is hard to sell at all. Customers rarely believe you when you tell them that it will be off and away in no time, once planted out. It also produces long arching canes so that a bushy specimen is unlikely to be produced. These are also annoyingly brittle so are easily snapped when brushed past or roughly handled. This has no long-term effect on the plant but when you pick one up and a large piece comes away in your hand you can be sure you have lost a sale.

All of this, plus the fact that it is rarely seen in gardens anyway so no-one asks for it, is enough to put off most nursery owners and even a pushy plant-lover like myself usually gives up the uneven battle to promote such plants. Just maybe after I have described the end result of your potentially brave purchase you may feel it worthwhile to come and take one of my scruffy youngsters off my hands.

In an appropriate position little more than a year or two after planting you should have an elegant arching shrub to 2.5 metres (8 ft) tall and wide. As most of its new canes arise from the base the only thing one has to do is to remove completely some of its older canes. This will allow room for new flowering wood to form and keep your shrub young and vigorous. Its arching stems are well clothed with rich green leaves up to 16 cm long by 7 cm wide ($6^1/4$ in by $2^3/4$ in). When they are young they are stained copper and they have large rounded stipules enclosing the stems.

The flowers, which are produced for a long season starting in late spring and finishing in autumn, consist of rich yellow trumpets in drooping racemes about 18 cm (7 in) long. These are followed by many-seeded green berries that look rather like gooseberries. I have doubts about using these fruit in the same way as gooseberries.

Our species comes from a genus of six shrubs in the Honeysuckle family, Caprifoliaceae, and was originally discovered by Frank Kingdon-Ward in 1928. In his book *Plant Hunting on the Edge of the World* he gave the following account of its discovery.

'On May 8th we started again up the valley, our object being to camp near the pass, not more than three days march, as we reckoned it. The river above Watersmeet was a roaring torrent, we were still high above it, but could often see it thundering through the gorge below. As for the path, it was a mere ledge high up on the rock face, with terrifying cliffs where we had to climb down shaky ladders forty or fifty feet high, holding on to roots and creepers. On a cliff, which was overgrown with shrubs, I found the golden *Leycesteria*, a solitary plant with long hanging racemes of golden-yellow flowers and large auricled stipules at the base of the leaves.'

After all Kingdon-Ward went through, it would be impolite not to grow it in our own gardens, don't you think?

The genus was named after William Leycester, Chief Justice of Bengal c.1820, who 'during a long series of years pursued

:very branch of horticulture with munificence, :eal and success'.

As it is not considered cold-hardy in :ngland it is usually recommended as a 'shrub :or the cool greenhouse' and was give an Award of Merit for this purpose in 1960.

Finally, you may well be familiar with *L. formosa*, a much more commonly grown shrub with white flowers surrounded by burgundy bracts. These are followed by purple berries much loved by birds; after a trip through their intestines, seedlings will often pop up in unexpected places. I haven't yet found the golden leycesteria to do this in my garden.

Lindera obtusiloba

How often have you seen a beautiful shrub or tree only to be disappointed when told that it wouldn't possibly grow for you? Probably quite often, I would think. This of course is a sweeping statement and if you are prepared to find or create the right aspect and conditions it is often surprising what can be grown. Think of the feelings of pride some supposedly impossible plant can engender if we succeed.

After all, the challenge of growing difficult plants can be part of the fun of gardening. Just don't get too depressed and start looking for a gas oven or the razor blades if it doesn't work.

It is also rather silly to fill our gardens with plants hard to maintain in our particular area. Just a few is normally enough to contend with. A garden full of flourishing easy-to-grow common plants is generally to be preferred to one full of struggling hospital cases that will make you feel guilty every time you go for a walk around your estate.

This shouldn't deter you from a bit of experimentation. I enjoy growing some subtropical plants in my cold Macedon garden and have been surprised by my success. My *Philodendron pinnatifidium* even came through the frosty winter of 1994 unscathed. Like most gamblers I won't tell you about all my losses that year but they were substantial and only to be expected; after all, my garden was to be open to the public late the next spring. I'm sure that many other gardeners came unstuck with Japanese maples and similar plants in the drought that followed.

This isn't, however, about subtropicals or for that matter tropicals. Instead, I want to tell you about a cool-climate shrub that I can grow very well indeed. If you don't live in a cool hill-station climate like mine, you may well struggle with it. If you decide not to give it a go, I hope that you will at least feel envious of my success.

My plant is *Lindera obtusiloba*, from the cool forests of Japan, Korea and China.It belongs to a genus of some eighty species, natives mainly of southern and eastern Asia with two coming from North America, and is related to the much tougher *Laurus nobilis*, the bay tree.

Although some *Lindera* are evergreen the most beautiful species, like my selection, are deciduous shrubs or small trees. They generally have aromatic foliage, befitting a genus in the Lauraceae family.

L. obtusiloba is a foliage shrub of the first order. Its large leaves are sometimes heart-shaped and entire, sometimes possessing two shallow forward-pointing lobes towards the tip or even with only one lobe on one side of the leaf. The effect of having various leaf shapes on one plant I find appealing and intriguing.

In spring the foliage is a wonderful fresh bright green and it holds this colour well into summer when many other plants have become quite sombre. It is however in autumn that *L. obtusiloba* leaves really become a star attraction. They turn a brilliant shade of yellow that few other plants can match and this is usually touched with a little bit of pinky-orange on just a few of the leaves.

If it is happy in your garden you could expect it to make an upright bushy shrub to about 3 metres (10 ft) after some ten years or so. Obviously a little bit of patience will be required but in the end you should be rewarded with a plant that everyone will admire. I know that my customers certainly do.

L. obtusiloba is dioecious, which means that male and female flowers are borne on separate plants, so you are not going to see its pea-sized black berries unless both sexes are present. Don't ask me for both, I have only a male plant and don't think I will bother to get a girl one.

The flowers are produced in late winter on the bare stems and consist (at least in the male form) of a cluster of stamens the colour of freshly made mustard. Individually they are no great shakes but in quantity look most attractive and if you could bear to cut them would look lovely as a cut flower.

If you decide to give one a go (assuming you can purchase one in the first place) select a sheltered site out of hot winds. It will be happy with morning sun or filtered light through a large tree. Make sure that the soil is lime free and full of lovely rich compost. Keep it well mulched and moist but not too wet. In fact if you can grow rhododendrons reasonably well you could put your *Lindera* with them.

Just a bit of trivia to finish with. It was introduced into Britain in 1880, received an Award of Merit for foliage in 1952 and the genus was named after Johann Linder (1678-1723), who was a Swedish botanist.

Loropetalum chinense

A plant of great charm and elegance that was better known years back than it is today is *Loropetalum chinense*, sometimes commonly known as Fringe Flower, not to be confused with the even more obscure Fringe Tree, *Chionanthus*. This second plant will probably always be on the fringe, due mainly to the difficulty of propagation. No such excuse exists for *Loropetalum*, which should be discovered and used by many more gardeners.

Before I move on, I must point out that the only thing *Loropetalum* and *Chionanthus* have in common is a common name. The first belongs to the Hamamelidaceae or Witch-hazel family and the second to the Oleaceae or Olive family.

Getting specific, *Loropetalum* is a small genus of probably two species, with only *L. chinense* found in cultivation. It is distinguished from *Hamamelis* by its small evergreen leaves and white flower. The shape and character of the two are also streets apart.

It is not considered to be fully hardy in England (what they mean by hardy is cold tolerance) but here in Australia we rarely have frosts hard enough to deal it a deathblow. Although it must be pointed out that late frosts on its new growth will give it quite a hiding.

What is more usually a problem with it in this country is excessive heat and dryness, so when selecting a site I would suggest a spot in morning sun or with filtered light (but not heavy shade) all day.

Lorapetalum likes a soil that is moisture retentive but not wet and although it doesn't need a highly acid soil make sure it is well enriched with organic matter and keep its roots well mulched.

So what is good about this plant?

Firstly, I would have to say that its growth habit is charming. It will eventually make a shrub about 2 metres (6 ft) tall and probably wider, with elegant arching branches well clothed with alternating rich green puckered and pubescent leaves.

If planted on a bank or the top of a retaining wall it will spill over in a most satisfactory way. If you don't have such sites that doesn't matter, it will look equally good tumbling over the ground.

Because of its drooping habit I could see it as a most effective espalier, informally trained up the wall to cascade back again. Grown this way it could easily be encouraged to greater heights than it would achieve on its own. My plant has comfortably over-topped a 2 metre (6 ft) paling fence and I'm sure it would have been more than happy trained up a metre more.

One point of warning if you do decide to encourage it to dizzy heights, keep in mind the brittle nature of the wood. That snapping sound created by excessive pushing and tugging is very depressing.

Another good way to show off its shape is to use it as a tub specimen. A well-grown plant in a large urn or barrel would look stunning in even the most fashionable quarters. I just hope it doesn't become so fashionable as to end up boringly common. I suppose this is one of the risks I take.

I haven't yet mentioned much about its crowning glory, the flowers. These consist of narrow strappy white petals and are usually grouped together in clusters of three to six. Individually they aren't up to much, but *en masse* they can cover the plant in tiny paper shreddings. They are quaint, appealing and showy in quantity and produced over quite a period from mid to late winter well into mid spring.

It is usually propagated by cuttings, which take a couple of years to reach plantable size and even then will be lying across the top of

he pot and over the edges, looking more like groundcover than a substantial shrub. This nay well explain its lack of popularity. We ursery people tend to get tired of explaining uch things all the time to practically every ustomer.

I have found mention of a pink-flowered orm in one of my books. I don't think I like he sound of it much as the new growth, vhich is often under way before the flowers inish, is a pale yellowy green. Not a combination that usually pleases me if the pink is a true rich one, and if it's not why have a pink one at all?

L. chinense was introduced by Charles Maries for Messrs Vietch in 1880 and received a First Class Certificate in 1894.

Finally, its name comes from the Greek *loron*, meaning 'thong', and *petalon*, 'petal'. I'm just glad the common name wasn't a literal translation as 'Thong Petal' doesn't sound very upmarket.

Luma apiculata

Until quite recently very few people knew or grew *Luma apiculata*, from South America. Its lack of publicity is probably to blame, although its changes of name may have had something to do with it.

The above-mentioned name seems now to be widely accepted but it can still be found sold as *Myrtus luma* or *M. apiculata* and has also been listed as *Eugenia apiculata* and even *Myrceugenella apiculata*, although I have never seen it sold under either of these last monikers.

The recent interest in *Luma* is due to the fact that it makes a remarkably good hedging plant. It will grow quickly to a screen of 3 metres (10 ft), responds to trimming very well and its small rich green leaves always look neat and dense. If all this isn't enough to get you out planting a *Luma* hedge then maybe the fact that it produces masses of lovely white flowers in late summer and autumn, when few quality trees and shrubs are blooming, should sway you.

Having said all this in favour of hedged *Luma*, I do think it is such a beautiful thing if left unpruned and grown as a small tree that to shape it is a little bit sacrilegious.

The reason I like to grow it as a specimen is due to its beautiful bark, which will not be visible if your hedge is dense, as all good hedges should be. If you are still determined to trim it perhaps you could grow it as a pleached allée and get the best of both worlds.

If you do plant just the one and grow it as nature intended, it will grow into a small multi-trunked tree to about 5 or 6 metres (16 ft 6 in to 20 ft), with a bushy rounded head. It will produce even larger crops of pure white flowers than if grown as a hedge and these will be followed by crops of edible black berries.

I find the fruit rather bland but the local birds, particularly the currawongs, love them. I regularly find self-sown seedlings obviously spread by the aforementioned currawongs.

I have put off discussing its star attraction (the bark) for long enough so here goes. The trunks of an established plant are sinuous, rather like those of an old olive tree, but the bark is smooth to look at yet powdery to the touch. Its basic colour is a rich cinnamon brown with a slightly green toning in it. This mature bark flakes off in patches to expose areas of white – a lovely piebald effect.

It must be a stunning sight in its natural habitat. A friend who has seen it in South America told me that it often grows in pure stands so thick as to exclude light reaching the ground so that nothing grows under it, and to wander amongst its tortuous trunks in the gloomy light was an eerie experience.

There are several mature *Luma* growing in gardens here in Mount Macedon, two of which are listed on the National Tree Register, and as I hadn't seen them growing in other areas I wrongly assumed that they were happy only in cold mountain environments. It is in fact a remarkably hardy small tree that will grow quite well in a variety of soils in shade or sun.

Although you may have to wait some years for the bark to develop its colour, cutting-grown plants of Cinnamon-barked Myrtle (as it is commonly known) will start to flower when quite small, which should keep you happy whilst you wait.

The only pruning that may be required for a non-hedged *Luma* is to completely remove some of its lower branches as it matures, so that you expose its lovely trunks to full view.

L. apiculata was introduced into England from its native haunts by William Lobb some time around 1844 and it received an Award of Merit in 1978.

The genus apparently consists of four specie

nd although I know nothing about the other hree I would love to give them a go if omeone has spare plants that they would like o donate.

The short but odd generic name of *Luma* is the native Chilean name for this tree and *apiculata* means 'terminating abruptly in a short and often sharp point'. This alludes to the leaves, which are pointed but definitely not sharp.

Magnolia dealbata

The genus *Magnolia* must contain some of the world's most spectacular flowering trees, and yet the blooms for all their size are quite simple and elegant in shape, avoiding even the slightest hint of vulgarity.

The simple floral structure suggests that they are among the world's most primitive flowering plants, and fossil remains would lead us to believe that they have remained relatively unchanged since earliest times.

The particular subject of this profile is surely one of the most exotic and historically interesting species of this remarkable genus. It is a rare plant from the cloud forests of southern Mexico and is listed as an endangered species. Its name is *Magnolia dealbata* and believe it or not it was the first species in the genus to be described in Western horticulture.

It was discovered by one Francisco Hernandez, Court Physician to Philip II of Spain, when he undertook the first scientific study of Mexico, commissioned in 1570. In 1651 members of the Academy of the Lincei re-edited some of the material brought back to Spain by Hernandez and published a picture of this magnolia under its Aztec name *Eloxochitl*, which is derived from 'elotl' (a green ear of corn) and 'xochitl' (a flower), apparently alluding to the flower bud. The name *Magnolia* commemorates Pierre Magnol (1638-1715), Professor of Medicine and Prefect of the Botanic Gardens at Montpellier.

Part of the reason for the rarity of *M. dealbata*, apart from its lack of hardiness in European gardens, is that the local inhabitants collect and sell the flower buds, which are used to decorate homes. The only way to harvest them is to cut down the tree as the buds are only produced on the ends of very brittle branches. This of course prevents the plant from setting seeds.

In 1975 an American expedition went to the plant's natural habitat, and although it can be expected to reach heights of up to 18 to 20 metres (60 to 65 ft), none were found to be above 9 metres (30 ft), as all were re-growths from older stumps.

Another interesting fact is that this is the only deciduous species from the tropics. Yet, perhaps due to its home being in the mountains, I have had no trouble in growing it at Mount Macedon.

My plant flowered for the first time at 2.5 metres (8 ft) in early December 1993, after only five years in the ground, much to my surprise and delight. It seems to like the same conditions as most of its relatives, that is a moist but well-drained soil and a position sheltered from strong winds.

However, don't get too excited at this point and rush out looking for one. They are hard to propagate and I have managed to get only a handful to strike, due to the thick wood being unsuitable for cuttings. These precious plants have ended up in the hands of a few very special customers!

Now I will finish with a few more statistics, to unfairly whet your appetites.

The leaves can grow up to 1 metre long (3 ft), though mine haven't grown to more than 50 cm (20 in) so far; the highly scented flower, at least from my one experience, is about 30 cm (12 in) across when fully open. Although my photograph shows a clear creamy-white bloom, in the wild populations it is apparently more usually marked with burgundy towards the centre. I should try to get that form as well, that would indeed be horticultural one-upmanship!

Mahonia lomariifolia

It is nice to have a plant that can truly be described as a wonderful foliage plant and yet still has other strings to its bow. Many such plants have flowers of little or no consequence, let alone pretty fruit.

Mahonia lomariifolia, from China and Burma, must rank as one of the finest of its genus, which is really saying something, and amongst the top contenders in the leaf brigade as a whole. Its very spiny leaflets are a rich deep green and produced in pairs of fifteen to twenty along the leaf stem, which can be 50 cm (20 in) long. These leaves radiate around stiffly upright stems in a bold architectural manner, creating a plant with enormous presence.

As the photograph shows, this is far from the end of the story. During autumn and early winter it produces long spikes of sweetly scented golden yellow flowers and these in turn are followed by handsome black berries with a faint white bloom, rather like some plums although nowhere near as big. The flower spikes can be up to 20 cm (8 in) long and consist of up to two hundred and fifty flowers, why not count them for yourself?

The berries have become quite popular with my band of local currawongs and of course the ever present blackbirds, which makes them something of a mixed blessing.

Culturally, mahonias pose few problems and require little more than a shady spot and moist but not wet soil. They will, in fact, stand quite a lot of sun but their leaves tend to yellow, which takes away from the autumn show as well as making them look as though they are lacking in vigour. This species can grow as a narrow plant up to 4 metres (13 ft) tall, reaching 10 metres (33 ft) in the wild, and will in time become bare at the bottom. I have nothing against bare bottoms in the right place but if they offend you then get out the pruning saw and some stout gloves and prune the whole plant to a stump in late winter, then off you go again. The job is even easier if a spouse or the undergardener is given the task.

I have now, in quite a purposeful way, led to the subject of prickly plants. Many of my customers are pointed in their objections to mahonias, as well as berberis and others. There are, on the other hand, some (allegedly) thornless roses but no-one ever suggests that these should be all that rose nurseries stock. This is a definite case of double standards, I would say. You may well find that there are locations in your garden where a prickly plant would be ideal.

Now for the mandatory dose of trivia. *Mahonia* is a genus of some seventy species from Asia, North and Central America, closely related to *Berberis* but distinguished from it by the thorny pinnate leaves without thorny stems. It was named after Bernard M'Mahon (1775-1816), an Irishman who fled to Philadelphia because of his involvement in a revolutionary plot. He was a friend of President Jefferson, and it is thought that the trail-blazing Lewis and Clark expedition to the Pacific coast was planned at his house. Jefferson gave a large part of his share of the specimens collected on the expedition to M'Mahon, who grew them in the botanic garden he had established in 1809. The genus was named by Thomas Nuttall, another member of the Philadelphia botanical circle.

The name of our species, *lomariifolia*, means that it has leaves like Lomaria (which has of course now had its name changed to *Blechnum*). *M. lomariifolia* was first introduced by Lawrence Johnston, of Hidcote Manor, as seed from Yunnan province in 1933. It received an Award of Merit for its foliage in 1938 and a First Class Certificate, again for foliage, in 1939.

In England much is being made of a group f hybrids between *M. lomariifolia* and 1. *japonica*, due mainly to them being more 'inter hardy than the first parent. These ybrids are not available here as far as I know, ut it would be fun to have plants with names ke 'Faith', 'Hope' and 'Charity', or the less)mantic 'Lionel Fortescue'!

Just to digress a little further, when the :lated *M. aquifolium* was first introduced from North America in 1823 it sold for the princely sum of ten pounds; this was reduced to five shillings by 1837 and by 1914 small plants were being offered at thirty shillings a thousand! In this day and age a comparable price, allowing for inflation, for a new introduction would be unthinkable. You could probably then have hired a gardener, with his wife thrown in to do the housework, for ten pounds a year. And some people say plants are dear today!

Malus trilobata

The genus *Malus*, which includes the domestic apples and crab apples, has for centuries been deservedly popular. After all what would life be like without a crispy juicy apple or a pot of tangy crab apple jelly? Over the years many new varieties have been developed or found as chance seedlings and with their current resurgence of popularity we now have literally hundreds to select from.

It is not however the apples but the crabs that I wish to have my say on here.

These are without exception hardy deciduous trees that will grow in many different soils and climates. As they rarely exceed 10 metres (33 ft) they make ideal shade trees for even quite small gardens.

Most have showy spring blossom although it must be remembered that the majority of those grown for their attractive fruit have less flamboyant flowers than the large double forms like *M. ioensis* 'Plena', the Bechtel crab. This one is so popular that it's a tad too predictable a choice.

I for one wouldn't be without at least one fruiting crab. They look so good in autumn, though often for a short time if the birds find them. If the birds don't get them I will, so they can end up in the kitchen or a bird's belly all to quickly.

If I was told I could have but one crab apple you might think that the choice would be difficult. I would have to do without *M. ioensis* 'Plena', with its pale pink confections in spring and lovely autumn leaves, but I could visit it in many other gardens. It might be harder to live without 'Golden Hornet', with its wonderful yellow fruit, or 'John Downie', which has perhaps the best-flavoured crabs, of a glowing orange red. But as the birds clean them up quite fast maybe a kind friend will supply me with an occasional jar of jelly, with the added bonus that my kitchen needn't become a sticky mess.

My choice would definitely have to be *M. trilobata*. It has everything you could possibly want in a small tree.

It is still quite rare, although it may not be the case when you finish reading this, making it a refreshing change from the obvious.

The tree is usually single-trunked with shortish laterals that give a neat conical shape to it. This means that it would be ideal in even a tiny garden.

Its leaves have three main lobes and these are also lobed, giving it more the appearance of a maple. This is a most desirable look, particularly in areas too hot too grow said maples. In spring the leaves are velvety and a silver green, by summer they are a rich glossy green and in autumn turn brilliant orange-reds, scarlets and burgundies, a definite challenger in the autumnal stakes.

The foliage is so different from its relatives that it is in a separate subsection of the genus and is sometimes put in a genus of its own called *Eriolobus*. It was even quite understandably once classed as a *Crataegus* (hawthorn).

In late spring it will cover itself in large single white slightly-scented flowers. These are usually about 3.5 cm ($1^1/2$ in) in diameter, a good size by anyone's standards, and have the charming simplicity often lost in doubles. As it blooms quite late in the season it gives a fresh spring-like look when many other blossom trees are past it and you may miss the worst of the spring gales that usually arrive in time to destroy the cherries' efforts.

The fruit are slightly pear-shaped and ripen to a soft yellow blushed with red. Because of its late flowering it rarely produces fruit in England but this shouldn't be a problem for antipodean gardeners. It should in fact be quite at home in many parts of southern Australia that are blessed with a climate close

ɔ that of its native haunts in the eastern ⁄lediterranean and western Asia, where ummers are often long and dry and winters ool to cold.

Linnaeus included the *Malus* in with the enus *Pyrus* (pears) but they are not known to ybridise or to graft one on the other at all well. 'hilip Miller (1691-1771), who was curator of ıe Chelsea Physic Garden for twenty-two ears, appreciated the differences and decided to ignore Linnaeus and wrote 'I shall therefore beg leave to continue the separation of the Apple from the Pear, as hath been always practiced by the botanists before his time'.

It is however interesting to note that *Malus trilobata* is one of the few crabs that produce fruit containing grit cells like those of pears. Let us hope this isn't enough to start the debate afresh.

Melanoselinum decipiens

As a child growing up in quiet Mount Macedon one had to make one's own entertainment. For me that usually meant being an explorer. I would set off in no particular direction with cut lunch in hand (this was usually consumed by midmorning as I didn't have a watch and had to rely on my stomach). The point of the excursions wasn't to get anywhere but to get to know the landscape, both natural and man-made, of my area. It would probably have come as something of a surprise to the owners of many of our old gardens that they had been playing unwitting host to a tiny Indiana Jones.

Even as a very young lad I had an interest in plants and I think my explorations helped reinforce my inclinations. Rescuing maidens from garden gazebos and fighting off bracken monsters would keep me busy all day and even now certain plants remind me of my pre-pubescent exploits. Like most youngsters, I was impressed more by bizarre and brash plants than by those that were merely pretty. After all it's far more fun to leap out of a clump of tropical-looking foliage pretending to be a muscle bound, monosyllabic loincloth wearer than to just smell the roses.

One plant that always impressed me and seemed to be a component of most of our old gardens was known only as Tree Angelica. No-one knew its botanical name and it didn't fit the description of any species of angelica in the reference books, but as a tropical-looking bold foliage plant it stood out in our cool damp gardens and is a major part of my childhood experiences.

Later research has shown it to be *Melanoselinum decipiens*, an umbrelliferous plant from Madeira, which the books call rather inappropriately Black Parsley. I will stick with Tree Angelica if I use a common name at all, it might well be only locally understood but the plant looks far more like this than a grovelling tuft of parsley.

The botanical name translates as 'black celery', which is nearly as bad, so perhaps we will just ignore that.

Visually this plant looks like an angelica on a palm trunk and usually grows to about 2.5 metres (8 ft), although I have seen specimens in shady gardens drawn up to 4 metres (13 ft). Each plant will have only a single trunk with the foliage at its top like an open umbrella. The trunk has rings of scar tissue evenly spaced along its length where old leaves used to be, making a very pleasing effect.

On a vigorous specimen the huge compound leaves can be more than 90 cm (2 ft 11 in) long and wide. Whilst young they are bronze tinged, are later bright fresh green and as they die they turn bright yellow then shed, leaving another trunk ring.

For some years this is all that will happen although I might add that this is quite enough to warrant garden space. When it decides to flower, which is the beginning of the end as *Melanoselinum* is monocarpic, a huge mass of tiny scented mauve-white flowers will erupt from the growing tip. Its family affinities will be obvious, as it looks like a giant trunked parsnip gone to seed. I have had specimens flower when less than five years old and know of others over fifteen that have yet to decide that enough is enough.

It is somewhat sad to see a large specimen dying after flowering and it can certainly leave a substantial gap in the garden but you can rest assured in the knowledge that next year you will have copious seedlings that will start the whole thing off again.

Like many of its relatives *Melanoselinum* resents disturbance, so if you intend spreading it around sow seeds in pots and then plant it in its permanent position whilst still small. In

ny own garden I usually sprinkle seeds where wish it to grow and then thin out any excess ater. The effect I usually aim for is to get a mall copse of plants, say three or five spaced vide enough to show off their arching :anopies. Individuals can often look a little ›dd and out of place unless surrounded with ›ther tropical-looking plants.

To grow it well, give it a sunny or semi-shaded aspect with a rich well-drained but never dry soil, then stand back and wait for the compliments to arrive.

Decipiens by the way means 'deceptive' or 'cheating', and I don't think it has anything to do with my childhood explorations and fantasies.

Mitraria coccinea

No garden could possibly be complete without climbing plants. It is so romantic to see whopping wisterias, rambling roses and cascading clematis rambling over fences and pergolas, clambering through trees and shrubs and covering walls with a soft blanket.

These plants evoke some of our most sentimental feelings about what a garden should be. But when it comes to the practicalities of climbers, the picture is far from rosy. They grow with remarkable speed, engulfing both the garden and the gardener in their exuberance, never do they grow in the desired direction nor stay in their allotted space.

So instead of the romantic look we often end up with lots of bare legs with all the flowers on the next-door neighbour's side or a series of unstuffed mattresses wobbling along the tops of our fences. Climbers require constant attention to keep them in bounds and the selection must be well thought out to avoid disaster and unrelieved drudgery for the rest of our lives.

When it comes to shady sites the problems become even more pronounced. Most climbing plants by nature run up looking for light so that bare legs are particularly prevalent. This is most depressing as instead of disguising the paling fence they tend to expose its unattractive self to all and sundry and do a lot of wobbling about the top.

If you have a shaded fence in a moist aspect then a plant you may like to try is *Mitraria coccinea*, from Chile and bordering parts of Argentina. It is really a clambering shrub so will need some wire or trellis through which it can be trained but as it produces no grabbing tendrils or twining stems it will stay nicely where it is put. When it reaches the top of the fence it will cascade back towards ground level and not tangle itself into a mess.

Although it grows quite quickly if happy, you will never be tangled in its embrace and nor will other plants that happen to be its bedfellows, all in all a most amenable scrambler. Its one drawback in the eyes of many gardeners is that its flowers are undeniably orange. Why so many people have an aversion to this colour is a mystery to me. It is always so cheery in a garden and will definitely brighten up a shady corner. Nor in the case of this plant does it make too bold a statement. Its individual blooms are inflated trumpets narrowing at the mouth, about 3 cm ($1^1/4$ in) long and are produced in moderate numbers over many months, starting in late spring and still going by late summer. They are set off well against the rich glossy green foliage, which is attractive all year round.

Specimens have been recorded up to 6 metres (20 ft), but it is rarely seen at even half this height and one would need a 6-metre wall anyway. I find it quite happy given average fence height.

If you haven't got space along a shaded fence it could be used to great effect in a fernery, or up a post under a pergola. It also makes an attractive cascading pot or hanging basket subject that is a little less predictable than the often-used fuchsias.

To propagate more stock just allow a branch to lie along the ground and it will root in a most satisfactory manner.

Its botanical name comes from the Latin word *mitra*, which translates as 'mitre', those pointy caps worn by bishops and the like.

I have mentioned most of its requirements already, i. e. shade and moisture. It also does best where the soil is acid and compost-enriched. If you are in a very cold area it could be a bit frost-prone although in its preferred aspect it is likely to be somewhat sheltered from the worst frost and unlikely to be damaged.

It was introduced to the famous Veitch Nursery of Exeter by William Lobb in 1846 and received an Award of Merit in 1927, obviously given by someone with no aversion to orange.

Neillia thibetica

Most plants have their season. All in all a fairly obvious statement, but gardeners tend to forget this all too often. When they visit a nursery and see something in full colour they are often carried away, take it home and realise at their leisure that it is attractive for only two weeks of the year. The rest of the time it's a mass of bare twigs or with dull boring foliage in summer.

I must admit that if I had something in my garden which flowered all year round, if I didn't actually end up detesting it, I would at least become blasé and never treat it with the respect it undoubtedly deserves.

What I like are plants that go through a succession of attractive changes throughout the year so that I can be restimulated again and again.

Not all these phases need be too overt and showy as long as I can enjoy the plant for as long as possible without the boredom of sameness.

One such stalwart garden shrub is *Neillia thibetica*. There isn't a time when I don't like this plant so I would say that it more than pays for its garden space. Let us then follow my *Neillia* through the year and discuss its features in chronological order.

The leaves are attractive mid green and alternate along the stems. They are lobed and nicely serrated with a textured finish. In early spring they break from their dormancy with pleasant coppery tones to the green, no better than many other plants in this respect but nice to see none the less.

By early summer we get into flowering season. At this time most of the rhododendrons have finished their hectic display and the hydrangeas haven't properly got into theirs. The individual blooms are tiny rose-pink trumpets and are produced in elegant slender racemes up to 15 cm (6 in) long. It continues its display till well after Christmas (in Southern Hemisphere gardens, for all my Northern readers). Although it never seems loaded with blooms their elegance makes this not only unnecessary but undesirable.

As the time of mellow fruitfulness progresses the flowers give way to interesting necklets of tiny seed capsules and in late autumn those lovely leaves that have been doing such a good job since early spring will turn a rich yellow before shedding.

With most plants that would be it for the year, but not with a neillia. In winter it has lovely copper-coloured arching canes with a zigzag pattern to the twigs. As for conditions, any well-drained but not dry aspect in sun or semi-shade will do, and a more useful filler for a border it would be hard to find.

It grows about 2 metres (6 ft) tall and will fill a gap about as wide. The only regular job required is to prune out old and spent canes after flowering in summer. If you can't stop at one plant, it is easily propagated from cuttings or by lifting rooted suckers in winter which are produced in small numbers.

It comes from a genus of some ten species in the Rosaceae family and is native to eastern and south-eastern Asia. The only other species available in Australia seems to be *N. sinensis*, which is white-flowered and to my mind distinctly inferior.

A.E. Pratt discovered it in 1890 and it was described as *N. longiracemosa* by W.B. Hemsley in 1892. In this interval, however, it was called *N. thibetica* by the French botanists Bureau and Franchet in 1891. Until 1963 the names were considered to belong to two species but Vidal sunk *longiracemosa* into synonymy.

E.H. Wilson introduced it into cultivation through the Arnold Arboretum, once in 1908 as *N. longiracemosa* and again as *N. thibetica*

in 1911, and it received an Award of Merit in 1931.

It was named after Patrick Neill (1776-1851), who was a Scottish printer and naturalist and Secretary of the Caledonian Horticultural Society.

I hope all the above has given you Neilla nough to convince you to try one.

Nyssa sinensis

Botanical names are a great mystery and stumbling block to many aspiring gardeners. If however you take the time to investigate their meanings you often find that they can tell you something about the plant, its habitat, its origin or its stature. If you spend some time doing a bit of detective work these discoveries can add much to your appreciation of any given plant. Many are of course commemorative names or are so old that their meanings have been lost in the mists of time. I for one wish that fewer plants were named after Russians and Poles. One can feel more than usually inadequate when trying to say *Paeonia mlokosewitschii* or *Scilla mischtschenkoana*.

Knowing the origins of a name, where the plant comes from and all the other trivia, not to mention practical information, can not only help us to grow it well but, just as with people we get to know, it gives our plant a personality. This is why I am so keen to include all this extraneous stuff in my writings.

One soon learns that not all taxonomists are dry boring scientists. Many of them obviously have (or had) the souls of romantics and poets, to say nothing of those that liked a good practical joke.

I would love to meet the people responsible for names like *Dracula* (a genus of orchids) or *Quisqualis*, which is a play on words for the Latin *quis*, meaning 'who', and *qualis*, meaning 'what'.

Uvularia, a dainty herbaceous perennial with pendant flowers, was named after the uvula, that lump of hanging skin at the back of one's mouth. No poet named this plant, but one of its common names is merry bells, which sounds much better, don't you think?

This is all leading to the plant in this profile, which is known botanically as *Nyssa sinensis*, or the Chinese Tupelo in common parlance.

If like me you haven't a classical education and a vast knowledge of Greek and Roman mythology, the name *Nyssa* may mean nothing. Could it perhaps be Latin for 'nicer', after all few plants have nicer autumn leaves.

Go out and buy yourself a good dictionary of plant names, like William T. Stearn's *Dictionary of Plant Names for Gardeners*, and you could look it up as well as getting hours of harmless pleasure checking the names of everything else you grow. Suddenly your garden will be filled with great deeds and wondrous facts all associated with your humble vegetation.

If you decide not to expend the funds to buy such a book I had best tell you that our plant was named after the water nymph Nyssa and this is due to the fact that many species prefer decidedly wet to swampy growing conditions. It may not be the best name association in the plant kingdom, but is a lot more romantic that some names I could think of for a tree that grows in bogs.

N. sinensis was discovered in China (*sinensis* means 'Chinese') by Augustine Henry, who described it as a rare tree occurring in mountain woods.

The first seeds were sent by E.H. Wilson to James Veitch and Sons' Chelsea nursery in 1901 or 1902 but apparently only one germinated. Even the professionals have these problems. If the accompanying photograph isn't enough to convince you to try *Nyssa sinensis* I had best describe its attributes to you.

It is an elegant usually conical to upright tree, not unlike a liquidambar in shape, and usually grows to around 15 metres (50 ft).

The leaves are usually about 15 cm (6 in) long, bronze-red tinged in spring, mid green in summer and brilliant shades of red in autumn. It received a First Class Certificate in 1976 and an Award of Garden Merit in 1984

or its autumn colour and must surely rank amongst the world's best autumnal trees. Its foliage usually holds well so that its period of glory can be longer than average.

Although other species of *Nyssa* are known to be water-loving and can be planted in damp conditions the Chinese tupelo seems to need no more than a fairly moist soil and will do best if the soil has a deep humus-rich admixture.

Make sure you buy your plant pot-grown or very small if you are offered one loose-rooted, as they resent too much disturbance.

If it does well for you I'm sure you'll agree there isn't much that's nicer than *Nyssa*.

Oemleria cerasiformis

Some plants really do get the run-around when it comes to names and it isn't any wonder that gardeners and nurserymen (and women) get frustrated with the changes that seem to be becoming more and more frequent.

The plant I have in mind has had more than its fair share of name changes since its discovery.

It was originally called *Nuttallia cerasiformis* in 1838 after Thomas Nuttall (1786-1859), a self-taught Yorkshire botanist and plant-collector who migrated to Philadelphia in 1808. It was named by fellow-botanists John Torrey and Asa Gray. Nuttall is also commemorated with such plants as *Cornus nuttallii*. Its name was later found to have been used for another genus of plants and so couldn't be accepted for our subject.

In 1841 the German botanist H.G.L. Reichenbach named it after his friend Augustus Gottlieb Oemler, a pharmacist and naturalist who spent most of his time in Savannah, Georgia. Oemler sent many rare plants home to Reichenbach and was also an acquaintance of Nuttall, Torrey and Stephen Elliott, another eminent botanist. Elliott and Torrey also have plants named after them, *Elliottia* (an ericaceous shrub) and *Torreya* (a conifer).

Torrey and Gray, realising their mistake in using the name *Nuttallia* but being ignorant of Reichenbach's decision, opted to rename it as *Osmaronia cerasiformis*. The new name must have taken quite some time to be accepted as the plant was given an Award of Merit in 1927 under its original name of *Nuttallia*.

In quite recent times Reichenbach's name for it came to light and after some discussion amongst the powers of botanical nomenclature it was at last decided in 1975 to go back to *Oemleria*, which had considerable precedence over *Osmaronia*. Let us all hope that this is the end of the story!

Now it is time to get on with the more practical aspects of what is clearly *Oemleria cerasiformis*, at least for now. If the botanical name (or names) are too much for you then perhaps you may like to stick with one of its two (yes, two) common names, these being Oso Berry or Oregon Plum. It is a monotypic genus in the Rosaceae family, closely related to *Prunus* although it doesn't look all that much like it.

There are both male and female plants and what I grow is by chance a male, which is the best to grow. The girl ones are supposed to be coarser of growth and not so free flowering although if I had one I would undoubtedly allow her to consort with my boy one for the sake of the large deep-purple plum-like fruit she would produce. These berries are reputedly very bitter and strongly almond-scented so one must wonder if they have more than ornamental value.

This deciduous shrub was introduced from its native Californian haunts in 1848 and although it is quite hardy and charming in a subtle way it has never become all that common or popular, maybe because no-one is sure what to call it.

One of its chief attributes is its upright habit, making it ideal where height is required but space is limited, or when you don't want something that will hang over and thus shade smaller fore-ground plants. Expect it to grow to 3 to 4 metres (10 to 13 ft) high by 1.5 metres (5 ft) wide.

The tiny white flowers and its lively fresh green foliage are both produced very early in the season, making it a herald of the more spectacular spring blossoms to follow. Although its flowers are quite small they have a dainty poise and an unusual scent, reminiscent of almonds, that makes this plant a most useful addition to the garden.

It is also a tough customer, not fussy about soil types or climate so any aspect from semi-shade to

full sun in a reasonably well-drained soil should suit it. I might add that it will obviously do even better if the soil has been worked on to improve its structure. After all, we all wish to have a garden full of thriving healthy plants and not a collection of things struggling to cope with their environment so that the garden looks more like a stress management clinic.

If it has a fault at all it may be its suckering habit. Many people have an aversion to plants that don't stay just where they are put. I must point out, however, that it is not vigorously suckering and this characteristic does give you an easy means by which you can increase stocks for use elsewhere or to give to deserving friends.

It is a shame that Nuttall, Torrey, Grey, Oemler and Reichenbach could not all get together over dinner and a glass of wine and sort the whole thing out a long time ago.

Oxydendrum arboreum

If you have often felt deprived because you lack deep rich acid soil in a cool enough climate so that you could have banks of rhododendrons, clusters of kalmias, copses of scarlet-leafed maples in autumn and all that richly diverse plant material from the forests and mountains of China, Japan and North America, then after reading the following you may well feel suicidal. On the other hand it may encourage you to at last buy that longed-for property in them there hills.

Oxydendrum arboreum, the Sorrel Tree or Sourwood, is one of North America's most stunning autumn aristocrats. The leaves, which can be up to 20 cm (8 in) long, are mid green from spring till autumn. It has a quite unassuming look to the leaf that would never prepare you for its grand finale.

As the cool nights arrive the leaves turn the most brilliant shades of cherry red to burgundy. Young potted plants in my nursery are snapped up by eager plant hunters and as often as not put back again after I describe its requirements.

It is called Sorrel Tree or Sourwood because the leaves have an acid taste and were used to allay thirst. But the sour looks I get as another one goes back into the shade house give a whole new meaning to the names.

Even its botanical name alludes to the taste as it comes from the Greek *oxys*, which means 'acid' or 'sharp', and *dendron*, 'tree'.

As if its autumn show wasn't enough the sorrel tree is no slouch in the floral stakes. Its flowers consist of drooping racemes of tiny slightly scented white lily-of-the-valley look-alikes. These racemes can be up to 25 cm (10 in) long and appear in mid summer when so many other trees are just greenery. It isn't uncommon for flowers still to be present as the foliage starts to turn.

Even when the flowers finish the seed heads, which are a grey-brown shade, still look effective and these will hang around until the winter wet and wind destroys them.

It can have either one or several trunks, which usually grow quite upright. At least as a young tree its laterals are well spaced and short, giving the whole plant a fairly narrow tiered look. As it ages the laterals generally become slightly pendulous and the crown of the tree broadens.

If you don't live in the hills and can't afford to buy there, but still wish to try an *Oxydendrum*, I had best lay it all out before you.

As mentioned before, a humus-rich well-mulched acid soil is required. This should be well drained but never dry. The aspect should be sheltered from strong wind and cool but not too dark, as this will inhibit flower set and rich autumn colour.

I find it performs well under 50 per cent shade cloth at least whilst it's young and hasn't hit the roof. In the wild it is recorded as having reached heights of 25 metres (80 ft), but in cultivation it rarely exceeds 8 metres (26 ft). Having said this, if you succeed at all in suburban coastal zones chances are that you will be doing well if it exceeds 2 to 3 metres (6 to 10 ft), and it would have to be some age to manage even this. It could well make a useful tub specimen.

Used as a companion for rhododendrons and azaleas, *Oxydendrum* has few equals. Its bird- and bee-attracting summer flowers and brilliant autumn hues will brighten things up when other plants can look a bit dull.

As it is in the Ericaceae family it has a fine fibrous root system, just like the related rhododendrons, so it won't compete unduly with its bedmates.

Sorrel tree was introduced into horticulture in 1752 so it has been around a while and its accolades include an Award of Merit for

autumn colour in 1951, an Award of Merit for flowers in 1957 and a First Class Certificate for autumn colour in 1972.

If your *Oxydendrum* looks set to break your heart, eat a few leaves first. They have been used to treat heart problems.

Parrotiopsis jacquemontiana

Do you live in an area where you can't grow *Cornus florida*, the beautiful North American dogwood? Perhaps your climate is a little too hot, a little too dry, or your soil too alkaline.

I am not suggesting that *Parrotiopsis jacquemontiana* will grown in the Nullarbor, but if you've struggled and lost the fight with *Cornus* perhaps you could try this beautiful but rare small tree. Its flowers do bear a passing resemblance to dogwood, especially if you don't look too closely. Although perhaps they may look a little like tiny *Romneya* flowers (Californian tree poppy), or maybe they look like what they are: *Parrotiopsis*!

The flower does have quite a lot in common with those of *C. florida* in that the true flowers are clusters in the centre and what look like petals are actually bracts. They are, however, not in any way related. *Parrotiopsis* is in the family Hamamelidaceae, with witch-hazels and liquidambars.

Our subject's generic name hasn't anything to do with avian loudmouths as my title may suggest, but comes from *Parrotia* (a related genus), the Persian ironbark, which itself is named after a German naturalist and traveller, F.W. Parrot (1792-1841), and the Greek *opsis*, meaning 'appearance'. It has much in common with *Parrotia* and was at one time included in that genus. To make matters more complicated it was once called *Fothergilla involucrata*, another small related genus.

The specific name of *jacquemontiana* commemorates the French naturalist Victor Jacquemont, who started his plant collecting expedition to the Himalays to distract his mind from an unfortunate love affair.

It was first discovered in Kashmir in 1836 by Dr H. Falconer, later Superintendent of the Calcutta Botanic Garden, but was not introduced until 1879, when seed was sent to Kew.

According to W.J. Bean's *Trees and Shrubs Hardy in the British Isles* its rough twigs were used for making rope bridges in its native habitat (this fine work is often a source of astounding trivia!). But I have decided against trekking in the Himalayas.

Let us now get to the important statistics of this beauty. It is a small deciduous tree, to about 6 metres (20 ft) tall, with spreading fan-shaped branches. The leaves are bright green, rather round and with serrated edges. They are generally about 6 cm (2^{1}/2 in) wide and turn a soft yellow before shedding in autumn. The flowers and bracts together are about 5 cm (2 in) across and although I must confess that they don't have the staying power individually of those of the dogwood, an established plant will often produce sporadic flushes throughout summer after the main spring flush is over. I am still (I might add) waiting for this to happen; my plant, after five or six years, has flowered for three years running, but so far only in spring, and has reached a height of about 3 metres (10 ft) and a spread of 2 metres (6 ft).

All my references, plus my own experience, suggest that a well-drained but not dry soil in a sheltered sunny aspect should be fine in all but the hottest climates, where an easterly aspect may be best.

Whether your soil is acid or alkaline doesn't seem to matter much, but I have found that a cooling mulch around the roots is a great help.

Finally, I hope my constant comparisons with the lovely dogwoods hasn't made you feel that this is but a poor second choice for the unfortunate people who can't grow dogwoods. *Parratiopsis* is a lovely and worthy small tree that has hidden its light under a bushel for far too long.

Philadelphus coronarius 'Aureus'

People who are new to gardening generally get excited by flamboyant plants. Things with big splashy flowers or boldly variegated foliage. As they mature, horticulturally speaking, they often become enchanted by dainty and subtle plants and combinations of plants. They then regularly become dismissive of their earlier enthusiasms and will definitely look down their collective noses at variegated leaves. If they are lucky, hopefully before they are too old to reap the benefits, they will come full circle and again start planting with an unrestrained hand.

During their tasteful phase variegated leaves will be seen as vulgar but I for one see nothing wrong with a little honest vulgarity, it can be a lot more stimulating than impeccable taste.

The one group of plants that have done more than any other to encourage us back to variegated leaves are the hostas. Even the most lily-livered gardener never sees hostas as crass.

Golden foliage plants haven't been quite so shunned but still have their detractors. However golden foliage used with some restraint can be a great asset, bringing a ray of sunshine to our gardens. It is somewhat unfortunate that so many golden-leafed shrubs actually need a fair amount of sun if they are to give the desired effect when it is the more shady aspects where our little rays of sunlight could be most telling.

Plants that grow well in shade usually have dark green foliage except for the gold-leafed forms of the aforementioned hostas.

One shrub that can be relied on to do its stuff in shade (as long as it's not really heavy shade) is *Philadelphus coronarius* 'Aureus'. It differs slightly in its floral parts from the green-leafed species so may in fact be a form of *P. caucasicus*, as many authorities are now suggesting.

The nursery trade being as it is will probably stick with *coronarius* for a long time so this is the name you will need if buying one

This golden-leafed philadelphus has lively yellow leaves, richest in spring but still attractively pale till autumn. In passing I must mention that to say something has yellow leaves (as this plant undoubtedly has) doesn't help it to sell as well as saying its leaves are golden. Off the top of my head, I can't think of a single plant that has truly golden leaves.

It requires some shade as its leaves will often scorch in bright sun, which will make it look tatty. This plant is however quite hardy and the more light it can get without scorching the richer the colour will be.

You can expect it to grow to about 2 metres (6 ft) tall and not quite as wide and the only thing it will need from you is the removal of old twiggy spent stems at ground level. This can be done at any time you like, although winter or spring pruning will reduce the number of flowers that season.

Speaking of flowers, I had best describe them. They are single and white, produced in late spring and early summer, and make little impact visually. They are however strongly scented, which makes up for any lack of show.

Many people believe the scent of the flowers is actually too strong for use as a cut flower, even John Gerard (1545-1612), the famous herbalist, complained about it in his quaint way and I quote: 'They have a pleasant sweete smell, but in my judgment troubling and molesting the head in a very strange manner. I once gathered the flowers and laid them in my chamber window, which smelled more strongly after they had lain together a few hours, but with such a pontick and unacquainted savor that they awaked me from sleep, so that I could not take rest till I had cast them out of my chamber.' To save a rush to the dictionary, 'pontic' is defined as 'having a somewhat sour and astringent taste, perhaps like Pontic rhubarb.'

The name *Philadelphus* possibly commemorates Ptolemy Philadelphus, an Egyptian king who ruled from 285 to 246 BC; literally translated, it means 'brotherly love'. Mock Orange is the common name and I used to wonder about its connection with sibling affection. But I have recently read that in Victorian times sprigs were sometimes used to take the place of orange blossoms in the wedding bouquets of country brides.

The genus *Philadelphus* has some sixty species native to south-eastern Europe and Asia Minor, North and Central America, China, eastern Asia, the Caucasus and the Himalayas. Our species was brought to Vienna from Turkey in 1562 (along with the lilac) by Ogier Ghiselin de Busbecq, Ambassador from the Emperor Ferdinand to Suleiman the Magnificent. There are innumerable varieties and cultivars and my selection received an Award of Merit in 1983 and an Award of Garden Merit in 1984.

Photinia beauverdiana

In many parts of Australia there is one large evergreen shrub that has been used for hedges and screens so often that in certain suburbs it tends to be almost the dominant species. The plant in question is *Photinia* 'Robusta', raised at Hazelwood's Nursery in Sydney many years ago.

It is so common that it hardly needs describing, but for those of you who don't know it by name I'm sure you will know what we are talking about if I tell you that it has glossy deep green foliage, bright coppery red new growth and flat clusters of slightly smelly white flowers, usually in spring. It makes a large bulky shrub that will often attain tree proportions and although it does make a dense screen that no neighbour could spy through, I happen to feel it is less than an inspired choice.

Things get even worse when you see this plant alternated with its partner in crime, *Pittosporum eugenioides* 'Variegatum'. This bulky bush is well known for its creamy-white margined, grey-green leaves. The overall effect when used together is like looking into someone's mouth after a trip to the dentist, a mass of bloody gums with regularly spaced teeth. I hope my graphic description may slow down the planting of such aberrations.

All in all, both plants can be damned with faint praise by describing them as useful.

So it comes as something of a surprise to people with this photinia aversion that I would ever recommend planting one. It won't of course be *P.* 'Robusta'.

When a plant is really common, people tend to assume (usually wrongly) that it is a fair representation of its genus.

Gardeners are often shocked when told there are deciduous daphnes (after all, *D. odora* is the only one usually seen in Australian nurseries) or climbing hydrangeas and so it is with photinias. I don't know of a climbing one but some of the deciduous photinias are truly lovely small trees that have been overlooked for far too long and I hope now to redress the situation.

The genus as it is now understood consists of some sixty or so species, including those plants once known as *Stranvaesia* and possibly *Heteromeles*. They can be deciduous or evergreen and usually make large shrubs or small trees.

P. beauverdiana is a lovely deciduous tree to about 8 metres (26 ft) tall and an established specimen will be attractive all year round.

In winter it makes an impressive silhouette with its branches arranged in drooping fans, usually fairly well spaced, and its bark is a nice smooth grey.

During early spring it will produce large heads of tiny white cotoneaster-like flowers. These do have the classical photinia smell, although I don't find it offensive; they are arranged across the tops of the branches and from a distance give the effect of collected snow. At the same time its leaves will be emerging and these start out copper-coloured with fine white fur and make an attractive foil for the flowers.

By mid summer the foliage has matured to a good mid green with a paler underside and by this time it is usually supporting large clusters of small red berries. These can still be hanging around well into autumn, birds allowing.

When autumn arrives we get another wonderful show, this time with brilliantly coloured foliage. The leaves will turn lovely shades of coppery-orange and scarlet with an occasional yellow tint thrown in for good measure.

Any tree offering such a constantly impressive show is to be encouraged. It is certainly not a one week wonder like so many more frequently planted specimens.

If it has any down sides at all it may be that it takes several years to flower and that it

doesn't like strong prevailing winds. It also can self-seed in cooler hill-station gardens but think of the free plants you will get. It is otherwise a hardy quick-growing plant, not fussy about aspect or soil, and grows to an appropriate size for even smallish gardens.

This native of western China was introduced by E.H. Wilson in 1900. It was named after Gustave Beauverd (1867-1940), a Swiss botanist and artist who was for many years in charge of the Barbey-Boissier Herbarium in Geneva. *Photinia*, by the way, comes from the Greek word *photeinos*, 'shining', which refers to the shiny leaves of some of the evergreen species.

If *Photinia beauverdiana* is still too big for your garden then perhaps you could try the similar *P. villosa* with its more upright vase shape and smaller leaves, flowers and berries. This is also a plant deserving greater attention.

Physocarpus opulifolius

The Rosaceae family contains some of the most beautiful and useful, not to mention hardy, plants for the garden or orchard. To most people it reached the pinnacle of success with roses. In fact it would be a brave garden writer who was prepared to say that he or she didn't like them, so I won't!

I am not, on the other hand, completely craven so with respect I would just like to suggest that perhaps some people are a little bit too preoccupied with the genus *Rosa*. I do of course have some roses but they are not allowed to dominate the garden. I like to keep things in proportion.

Other genera in Rosaceae for which I have a fondness include *Sorbus* (rowans), *Crataegus* (hawthorns), *Malus* (crab apples) and *Pyrus* (pears). I couldn't afford to collect any of these groups as I garden on a smallish scale but I certainly have at least one of each. They may not (to some people) be as romantic as a rose but I adore them.

An even more obscure genus in this giant family which is even less likely to be awarded 'Shrub of the Year' is *Physocarpus*. It is a group of some ten species of deciduous shrubs from North America, Mexico and north-eastern Asia.

The only species you are likely to meet in Australia is *P. opulifolius*, from North America. This rarely grown shrub may not be as showy as a rose but in my humble opinion it is an attractive and valuable workhorse that should be used more.

So why should you consider planting one?

To start with, it is tough and quick-growing and requires virtually no attention although you could completely remove older canes occasionally if you felt like it. This reliability could only be seen as a disadvantage by those who feel things are only worth having if they are hard to keep.

It can be grown in full sun or part shade in pretty well any sort of soil and is almost embarrassingly easy to propagate from cuttings, layers or seeds.

The overall shape of the bush is elegant as its canes, which can reach up to 3 metres (10 ft) in rich soils, arch over at the ends.

In winter the bare canes will make a pleasing picture with their arching habit and the fact that the bark on the younger canes is a pleasant coppery colour. At this point I might mention that the common name for this shrub is Nine Bark. It is supposed to shed its bark nine times in a year. This I doubt but haven't bothered to check for myself.

When the leaves appear in spring they are a good rich green, three lobed and looking something like those of a flowering currant although prettier. In autumn they usually turn a respectable yellow, often tinged orange.

If this isn't enough for you, buy *P. opulifolius* 'Luteus', which has clear yellow foliage in spring that greens a bit in summer. I have also seen plants labelled as *P. opulifolius* 'Darts Gold'; these are supposed to stay gold throughout the summer, although I have a sneaking suspicion that all the gold ones in Australia are in fact 'Luteus'.

In mid to late spring it produces tight clusters of small white hawthorn-like flowers and these are followed in turn by papery coppery-pink seed pods. Both its flowers and pods are useful for indoor decoration, just remember that picking quantities of flowers will give you less pods for later.

So if you are looking for a hardy shrub to use at the back of a border or something that can be left to its own devices in a wild part of the garden, which is unlikely unless you have a grand estate, you could do a lot worse than selecting *Physocarpus opulifolius*.

Piptanthus nepalensis

I find that plants with glossy rich to deep green leaves (especially if they are attractively shaped) combined with flowers of a clear bright yellow make a cheery and arresting sight.

Bright though this combination is it doesn't clash or jar and as long as you like yellow in the first place, and I find some unfortunates don't, then you should be considering *Piptanthus nepalensis* syn. *P. laburnifolius*.

Before I go on to sing the praises of this underused and almost unknown shrub, I feel a need to discuss certain colours. Those of you who dislike or won't use particular colours are truly deprived folk. This aversion cuts you off from so much good plant material. If you can find no rational reason for it then plant something outrageous and try some shock therapy. The great mass of orange and magenta haters that outnumbers all other colour-shy groups please take note. Not of course that I am suggesting mixing orange and magenta together, but do so if you feel the need.

Now back to *Piptanthus*. It is usually described as a genus of two species, one with tomentose (furry) leaves, appropriately call *P. tomentosa*, and our selection, *P. nepalensis*, which has shiny non-hairy adult foliage. I must point out that the emerging leaves are somewhat pubescent.

Some authorities suggest that there may be as many as eight species but I don't know if they are additional ones unknown to the these authorities. Perhaps some taxonomists divide up what we have into more species due to minute variations.

Piptanthus is sometimes known as Evergreen Laburnum. It is somewhat ridiculous to use some other plant's botanical name as a common name when this shrub has a perfectly good and pronounceable one of its own. Besides, although *Piptanthus* and *Laburnum* are both legumes (in the Pea family) and they both have yellow pea flowers and trifoliolate leaves (divided into three leaflets) they don't really have that much in common, although you may think this is more than enough to be going on with.

Probably the major difference is in the flowers. As is well known, *Laburnum* has long drooping racemes of rich yellow flowers in late spring. *Piptanthus* has flowers of a richer yellow which are about twice the size, but in short more or less upright spikes to 15 cm (6 in) long, and they are there for months instead of weeks.

This would seem an appropriate point to explain the meaning of its botanical name. *Piptanthus* comes from the Greek words *piptein*, which means 'to fall', and *anthos*, which is of course 'flower'. The books tell us that this name is due to the fact that as the flower finishes it sheds the calyx, corolla and stamens in one piece leaving a naked pea pod.

Apparently my plant hasn't read the appropriate literature as its calyx seems to shed well after the rest has gone.

The foliage of *Piptanthus* is lovely. At about twice the size of *Laburnum* and a wonderfully glossy rich green instead of a dreary matt finish, it is attractive in or out of bloom. In cold climates it can be somewhat deciduous but it is evergreen in most areas of Australia that suit it.

Now to some specifics. It is a very quick-growing shrub, often reaching its full height of 3 to 4 metres in as many years (10 to 13 ft).

Plant it in a sunny well-drained aspect with moderately fertile soil and stand back. It does not like to be moved or planted too big so start with a young pot-grown plant. It is usually grown from seed, which like so many others in this family is best soaked in warm water overnight before sowing. If by morning the seed hasn't swollen up, the water probably wasn't warm enough so try again with it hotter.

Unlike many legumes if it gets lanky or old and woody it can be coppiced well down and will break away again from the stump. I must point out, however, it is often not very long lived so it is probably best to start off a new plant from seed if yours is getting on a bit.

Throughout its life prune out older spent canes and twiggy woody material right down to the base. This will encourage strong watershoots and retain its natural shape. Never trim it with shears; it won't make a dense blob and you will encourage a twiggy plant that with loss of vigour will flower less.

Piptanthus was introduced from the Himalayas, where it grows at up to 3,600 metres (11,800 ft) elevation, in 1821 and received an Award of Merit in 1960. It obviously took some time to get itself noticed. I can't understand why with its brilliant green and gold livery.

Pittosporum tobira

The genus *Pittosporum* is a large one consisting of some two hundred species native mainly to Australia and New Zealand. They can also be found throughout the Pacific region up through Malaysia into Korea, Japan and China as well as Africa. There is also one rare species from Madeira and one in the Canary Islands. They are all evergreen shrubs or trees mostly very hardy in our Australian gardens. One species native to Victoria, *P. undulatum*, has even become something of a noxious weed in areas of Australia where it is not endemic. It has also naturalised in the Azores, where it was introduced in the nineteenth century as a shelter tree for the orange groves.

Most are pleasant enough foliage shrubs, some of which like *P. eugenioides* 'Variegatum' and *P. tenuifolium* 'James Stirling' are grown in vast quantities by the nursery trade in this country. In my humble opinion their numbers far exceed their ornamental value. Many have a very nice perfume whilst in flower although they are rarely visually exciting. The flowers are usually small, often hidden amongst the foliage and generally of sombre colours.

There is however one species native to Japan, Korea and China that has not only a fabulous perfume but quite showy flowers and impressive foliage to boot. This most useful species is known botanically as *P. tobira* and why it hasn't superseded *P. eugenioides* or the ubiquitous 'James Stirling' is a mystery to me.

It was introduced into England in 1804 and has been available in Victoria since at least 1857, when it was listed by T. Adcock of Geelong in his catalogue of that year, so although it is something of a rarity it is not really new.

In 1984 it received both an Award of Merit and the even higher accolade, an Award of Garden Merit, from the Royal Horticultural Society and it is planted in large numbers in many of the world's Mediterranean climates, excluding our own.

As it is tolerant of shade or sun, fairly drought-proof, unaffected by salt spray and not prone to any major pest or disease, why has it been hiding for so long?

The foliage is a rich deep green, glossy and blunt tipped, and it makes an admirable screen or hedging plant. As it can be pruned quite hard its eventual size of 5 metres (16 ft 6 in) or more needn't discourage you from planting it even if your plot isn't large.

In late spring and early summer it will produce sizeable clusters of creamy-white flowers that will gradually age to a soft yellow. These are set off well against the leaves, which surround them but never hide them. The scent is strong and citrus-like but never overbearing or cloying, and will waft on the air for some considerable distance. I find in my own garden that it has few if any competitors amongst the ranks of flowering evergreens at this time of the year. Those who like even more colour may well opt for its silver-variegated form, predictably called *P. tobira* 'Variegatum', although I find its foliage competes for attention with the flowers.

There is even a dwarf compact form called *P. tobira* 'Wheelers Dwarf', which rarely exceeds 60 cm (2 ft) and makes a neat rounded bun. I have seen this sold here under the disgusting name of 'Little Miss Muffett' with a giant label complete with aforementioned lass and attendant spider. Apart from this offending promotional name I have one other reservation about this selection. Although it has made a respectable tuffet in my garden after several years, it has yet to flower and I haven't been able to find out if it is just slow to get going or even worse a non-flowering cultivar. Perhaps you know and would be kind enough to tell me.

Plectranthus argentatus

As our gardens get older and trees larger we nearly all start having problems with dry shade. Plants that once flourished in our little sun pockets start to lose vigour as overhead branches encroach. All in all, our pride and joy starts to look rather ratty.

Some relief can be gained by thinning out the branches of large shrubs and trees or we can even take the radical step and completely remove some of the worst offenders. I know that the removal of large and often well-loved trees is a traumatic experience but one must consider the needs of the garden as a whole and most of us do tend to over plant. Not in itself a bad thing as long as you can be ruthless later on. Just remember that you have to break an egg to make an omelette.

Having said all this, we obviously don't want to follow the scorched earth policy so we will still have some shady deserts to deal with.

When you start looking for plant material that will cope (or even more importantly flourish) in these aspects you will find that a high proportion of candidates will be what are loosely called foliage plants. This doesn't mean that they don't flower, most do, but that the floral display is secondary to that of its leafage.

Another aspect that will soon become apparent is that many of these plants will have foliage in the rich dark green shades so that plants with different colours are quite precious.

Before I launch into describing one of my favourite loves, I would like to sound a warning to all intending to purchase any plants for dry shade. The nursery will probably be growing its stock of such plants under shade but they will be feeding and watering more heavily than these plants will get when you take them home. It is important therefore that they are weaned gradually. For at least the first summer, water well and feed regularly until their infant roots have got a good hold. You can't expect a newborn baby to be self-supporting.

Plectranthus argentatus is the only truly silver-foliaged evergreen plant I know of that will grow well in such conditions.

It is an Australian native that grows naturally on rock ledges in the coastal ranges of south-eastern Queensland and adjoining areas of New South Wales.

On seeing it for the first time most people are surprised that it is a native. This might seem strange but many people tend to have a somewhat narrow view of our indigenous flora. It must be admitted that a high proportion have foliage that is hard and dry or small and feathery, and the large felty succulent leaves of *P. argentatus* don't fit into what is perceived as the classic mould.

This quick-growing shrub will attain its full stature of about 1 metre (3 ft) tall, with a width that exceeds its height, in just one growing season.

The leaves, which are up to 11 cm by 6 cm ($4^1/2$ in by $2^1/2$ in), look as though they have been made from silvery blue satin. They are heavily veined and slightly serrated, supported on thick succulent stems that often have a mauve colour.

If it did nothing else I would consider it a plant of distinction but as the summer wanes it starts to produce flowers that are a well-orchestrated symphony in combination with its foliage. The flower stems and floral bracts are a lovely rich mauve, setting off the small blue-white flowers to perfection.

These flowers can be produced well into winter so the display is quite prolonged, as long as it doesn't get caught by a frost.

Although it is frost-tender, I find even in my cool climate that I rarely lose it. Just let it alone and ignore the tattered mess until spring. Then cut it back hard and away you go again.

Alternatively, start some cuttings in summer or early autumn in a sheltered spot like a verandah or sunroom and these can be bedded out in spring to replace the old ones. They are as easy to strike as fuchsias or pelargoniums so shouldn't tax any half proficient green thumb.

Although I have recommended *P. argentatus* for shade it will grow equally well in more sunny aspects and also makes a lovely pot or hanging basket subject so you may not be able to stop at one.

Finally, the mandatory trivia. *P. argentatus* belongs to a genus of about three hundred and fifty species native to Africa and Asia as well as Australia. This genus includes annuals, perennial herbs and shrubs and belongs in the Mint family, *Labiatae* or *Lamiaceae* depending on whose book you follow. The genetic name comes from the Greek *plectron*, 'a spur', and *anthos*, 'a flower', which alludes to the fact that many species have a corolla with a basal spur.

Prunus serrula

If the accompanying picture of *Prunus serrula* excites you, read on.

This lovely tree was introduced into England in 1908 by Ernest Henry Wilson, best-known of the many distinguished plant collectors who worked for the Chelsea nursery firm of James Veitch and Son. He is usually known, rather formally, as E. H. Wilson and less formally as 'Chinese' Wilson, in recognition of the counry where he made some of his most important discoveries. He later became Director of the Arnold Arboretum, which is connected with Harvard University.

P. serrula received an Award of Merit in 1944 for its bark. Like most of the *Prunus* species it is not particularly difficult to grow and will quite quickly make a small spreading tree, growing to about 8 metres (26 ft). Some pruning of lower branches is desirable to expose the stunning trunks, but apart from this no regular lopping is necessary.

It has narrow willow-like foliage of a mid green colour and tiny white blossoms in spring with the new foliage. Neither flowers nor leaves are impressive but don't let that put you off; many trees are planted for their bark alone.

When selecting a site for this tree (commonly called Tibetan Cherry) make sure that the winter sun will catch the trunks and that it is close to a path so you can stroke it as you pass. Not only will you gain great pleasure from caressing its smooth sensuous limbs but if you are caught in the act you can quite rightly explain that rubbing the stems keeps them clean of moss and algae and makes the bark all the shinier.

The only real problem I have with Tibetan cherry is the dreaded pear slug, which can soon turn the leaves into grey skeletons. Although these pests will make the foliage look quite wretched they don't seem to retard growth much, so they are more a nuisance than a real problem. If you don't like using poisonous sprays, and can't learn to ignore pear slug as I have, try covering the tree with dry dust – talcum powder, lime or the insides of the vacuum cleaner will do. Pick a calm day then stand back and watch the slugs shrivel up as the dust dries their slimy little bodies.

Another point to keep in mind is that *P. serrula* is usually budded onto a normal cherry understock; just make sure when you plant it that the union is at ground level so that the different-coloured bark is not visible.

I hope that you will now want to rush out and buy one of these magnificent trees, which could well turn a French polisher green with envy.

Pseudocydonia sinensis

If you are looking for a small ornamental tree that is hardy, picturesque and multipurpose (in fact the perfect tree), I have a suggestion for you. Try *Pseudocydonia sinensis*.

It is always difficult to select a major specimen plant for a small garden. There are just so many factors to consider.

Let us now see how well this lovely tree can stack up when compared to what I think is a fairly comprehensive set of requirements.

When we select any major plant its hardiness must be of prime importance. Can it stand heat and drought as well as cold, poor soil and exposure to wind?

Pseudocydonia, or Chinese Quince as it can be called, will tolerate the coldest we have to offer in Australia and yet once established will be quite heat- and drought-proof. It can cope admirably with poor soils and only resents a wet waterlogged site. This doesn't mean that it wouldn't appreciate richer fare, so spend a little time improving your soil with copious amounts of organic material and the plant will respond to your solicitude.

Eventual size can be important, although just how big a tree should be in a small garden is to some extent dependent on one's own taste and requirements. Some poor souls feel that nothing should grow above their spouting. These people don't really want trees at all but would be better to stick with shrubs that have delusions of grandeur. Others will be happy only when they have created an urban forest in which Hansel and Gretel could get lost. Overly large trees do have inherent risks. Their roots may lift your house off its foundations or at least create friction with neighbours who don't like the shade as much as you do.

Chinese quince is usually a nice medium-sized tree growing to about 6 or 7 metres each way (20 to 23 ft), although it is supposed to get to 12 metres (40 ft) or so in the wild. I imagine we'll be two metres under well before it reaches this lofty height.

How long during the year a plant gives colour or at least remains attractive is very important. A major feature plant can't be a one week wonder unless you have acres to spare.

So how well does our selection do in the ornamental stakes?

It starts the season by producing soft pink flowers in spring with its newly emerging pale green leaves. As the season advances the foliage becomes a rich deep green and the plant will be studded with 10 to 15 cm (4 to 6 in) pear-shaped green fruit. By mid autumn the leaves will begin to turn rich shades of yellow, orange and scarlet at the same time as its decorative fruits turn yellow.

If all of this is still not enough to satisfy you, look forward to it attaining some age because as it matures it will have a rugged appearance like an old olive tree or mulberry and produce lovely plate-like exfoliating bark not unlike that of a crape myrtle.

For those of a practical bent the fruit can be used in the same ways as that of the normal quince, to which it is closely related. So think of all that lovely jelly and paste in your larder.

Pseudocydonia has at various times been included in the genera *Cydonia* (true quince) and *Chaenomeles* (flowering quince or japonica). These name changes may have something to do with its obscurity. Its present genus is monotypic.

It is relatively easy to propagate from seed or by grafting onto ordinary quince understocks and as far as I can tell it has no vices or down side to its spotless character.

In 1974 Richmond E. Harrison, of the famous New Zealand Nursery, Harrison's, in his *Handbook of Trees and Shrubs* said 'This sadly overlooked tree is a most useful subject

.s a specimen tree'. He listed it as *Chaenomeles inensis*.

It was introduced into England in the last lecade of the eighteenth century but was after-vards lost to cultivation and re-introduced from taly in 1898. It is not truly hardy in England and refers a more Mediterranean-style climate. This nay in part explain its rarity status.

Pseudocydonia comes from the Greek for 'false' and *cydonia* for the town of Cydon (now Khania) in Crete, where the best quinces were supposed to come from.

The species name sinensis refers to China. The Chinese were vaguely known to the ancient Greeks and Romans as the Sinai or Sinae.

If I have got you inspired and you can't make room for *Pseudocydonia* you may even like to espalier it on a sunny wall.

Pterostyrax hispida

Pterostyrax hispida, the Epaulette Tree, is a quick-growing and handsome plant from China and Japan that could be a worthy candidate for any sheltered garden, be it large or small.

In the Southern Hemisphere it flowers in December, at just the right time to carry on the garden show after the last hectic spring flourish is over. This is also probably part of the reason why it is not often planted, as most gardeners have finished their spring buying and so don't get to see my stunning 4 metre high (13 ft) specimen in bloom. Less fortunate nurserypeople find it even harder to sell; it rarely flowers as a small plant in a pot, and it is grown in such small quantities that pictorial labels don't exist.

In the wild it is a spreading deciduous tree to 13 metres (43 ft) tall by half as much in width, but in cultivation it is rarely seen over 8 metres (26 ft). So it makes an ideal small shade tree. It needs shelter from strong winds, mainly to stop its 20 cm (8 in) leaves from being ripped. Any well-drained and mulched soil should suit. It is rarely seen outside the Dandenongs and other hill-station areas, but I think this is due more to the fact that so many knowledgeable and keen gardeners flock to such areas than that *Ptserostyrax* can be grown only there. It will probably take only a few lowlanders to take the risk to prove me right.

As can be seen from the photograph, the epaulette tree has drooping panicles of tiny white flowers arranged with military precision. What is less obvious is that these same panicles can be 23 cm (9 in) long and the blooms exude a slight but pleasant scent.

After flowering, the branches of the panicles curl in towards the main stem and support small green bristly seeds that slowly turn light brown at about the time the leaves turn a soft pale yellow. Even the skeletal drooping panicles on the bare winter limbs can still make a good conversation piece.

The shaggy grey bark of an established specimen has a slightly fetid smell when crushed. As this does neither you nor the tree any good I wouldn't recommend it.

P. hispida is the only species of its genus grown in Australia as far as I know, and is the largest-growing of the three to seven species (the number seems to depend on what reference book you are using). All are native to Burma, China and Japan, and our subject was introduced into England in 1875; it rather belatedly received an Award of Merit in 1964.

Its name comes from the Greek *pteron*, 'a wing', and *styrax*, which is a related genus, so roughly translated it means 'a wing-fruited styrax'. The species name *hispida* means 'bristly', a reference to its seed capsules. The only other aspect that needs to be mentioned is that young trees will often branch rather low down, and although multiple trunks are quite in order much of this lower branching should be removed. This will lift the canopy up to eye level and above, thus allowing the flowers to be viewed properly as well as making room under it where you can sit and reflect.

Quercus rubra 'Aurea'

'Great oaks from little acorns grow', but if you like the idea of a golden-leafed oak then buy one that has been grafted.

The best-known golden oak is *Quercus robur* 'Concordia', the Golden English Oak, and a beautiful though very slow plant it is with its rich golden yellow leaves from spring till autumn. If you decide to buy one (as well you might) be warned that too much sun is likely to scorch its lovely leaves and too little is likely to turn them pale green. From specimens I have seen, it would seem to be potluck finding just the right aspect. Some I am acquainted with are doing well in aspects I would have thought too sunny. I suppose that this is yet another example of the unpredictability of gardening.

A second golden oak that is sometimes met with in Australia is *Q. rubra* 'Aurea', the Golden Red Oak, which sounds like a contradiction if ever I've heard one.

It is a far more vigorous plant than its English counterpart, but like most things in life there is a down side. Although in spring its large leaves are a stunning soft yellow that could easily compete with the yellow flowers of this season they will fade to light green in summer, looking no different from the foliage of the wild species in the woods of eastern North America.

It may however turn better colours in autumn than the golden English oak but don't expect it to go bright red as the other part of its name would suggest. There are definitely oaks that deserve the title of 'Red' more than this one.

Like most golden forms it tends not to be as vigorous or large growing as its green form but can none the less make a sizeable specimen tree, so is probably not suitable for small gardens unless all you want is one tree.

If it can be planted against a dark background it will undoubtably be the crowning glory of your spring display.

It was first discovered in Oudenbosch, Holland, in about 1878 and it is reputed that a percentage of golden ones can be had from seed. This isn't likely to happen for a while in the antipodes as I don't think it has been here long enough to set acorns. I would still opt for a grafted plant if given a choice as seedlings will be variable anyway.

The Hillier Manual of Trees and Shrubs suggests that two forms are grown under this name but it doesn't say how they differ. One must assume that if seedlings do in fact throw some golden plants they are all separate clones, so there may well be multitudinous forms.

I might add at this point that due to the fact that oaks aren't the world's easiest plants to graft, if you do find a *Q. rubra* 'Aurea' for sale don't be too surprised by the price. Gold has always been valuable anyway.

It isn't a fussy tree and will grow well in most soil types and is not affected by cold. Even the gold form is quick growing, at least by oak standards, so shouldn't take too long to reach a reasonable size. Unlike many oaks it will transplant quite well so if yours is getting too large for your tiny garden, you could lift it and give it to some deserving friend on broad acres and start off another small one.

The oaks have long been considered symbols of strength and were sacred to those two butch gods Jupiter and Thor. Druids thought that oaks inspired prophecy and built their altars under the canopy. I would suggest a garden seat from which to contemplate would be a good modern equivalent. Sacrificing virgins will certainly upset the neighbours and is probably against council regulations.

If you decide not to plant my selection then you could well look amongst the other six hundred or so species of *Quercus*. I'm sure you will find something you would like.

Rehderodendron macrocarpum

Even the greatest plant collectors must have missed many a good plant when exploring uncharted territory. One of your guides may well have been asking if you wished to have tea made just when you should have looked up. Perhaps you were too busy dealing with hostile natives or large carnivores to be paying attention to the local flora or were just not up to it after your last bout of dysentery.

Amongst the elite plant collectors was E.H. Wilson, who lived from 1876 to 1930 and did most of his collecting in China. He is responsible for first introducing such notable plants as *Acer griseum, Berberis wilsoniae* (a prickly customer to name after his wife), *Rhododendron williamsianum* and *Viburnum davidii*. This is but a sprinkling of the garden-worthy things this remarkable man has given us.

Imagine how he would have felt if he'd known that a completely unknown genus was within his grasp, a lovely one at that, and he'd walked under it and away leaving it to be discovered in 1931, a year after his death. He did just that on Mount Omei, in western China, when he missed the possibly endemic tree *Rehderodendron macrocarpum*.

It was left to a local botanist, Mr F.T. Wang, to discover it. It is named after Dr Alfred Rehder (1863-1949), of the Arnold Arboretum, and it was here that the first seeds were raised in the Western world. These were sent in 1934 by Professor H. Hu, who named the genus.

It now appears that *Rehderodendron* belongs in the Styracaceae family. The genus consists of nine or ten species of deciduous shrubs and trees, mainly from China but with one from Indo-China. At least in the species under discussion here it is as good as or better than practically anything else in this family. This I might add is really saying something.

Visually this small tree has a lot going for it, so let's see just what its assets are.

It will make a small conical tree to 7 metres (23 ft) tall with almost horizontal branches. Plants of this shape always look good, I feel.

The attractive finely serrated leaves are about 10 cm (4 in) long and usually turn brilliant colours of red and orange in autumn. This is something that its relatives such as *Styrax* and *Halesia* don't usually manage. Another bonus is that the new twigs and petioles (leaf stems) are rich red all season. This isn't a major asset but a useful additional bonus.

Its flowers are charming drooping bells that are usually white, although pink forms are known. They are produced in clusters below the branches in spring after the foliage has made its appearance. The blooms are slightly lemon-fragrant and contain conspicuous yellow stamens.

The excitement doesn't finish here. After the flowers shed it produces quite large pendulous woody fruits. These are oblong in shape with eight to ten ribs and bright red. Every bit as good as flowers and they last a lot longer. What more could anyone possibly want?

Now we had better discuss cultural requirements seeing that I've probably got you worked up enough to grow one. *Rehderodendron* requires a lime-free moist humus-rich soil in a sheltered aspect, well protected from hot winds and afternoon sun. In fact much the same sort of conditions required by all rhododendrons and azaleas, which you probably can't grow either.

Don't let it get to you, as you probably won't be able to get one to lose anyway, but you are more than welcome to come and visit mine the next time you are passing.

It is plants like this that keep me hoping that I might some day find some wonderful thing that more experienced plant hunters missed before me. Perhaps there will some day be a *Ryania superba*.

Rhaphithamnus spinosus

I don't usually complain when a botanical name is descriptive, after all if it tells you something about where a plant comes from or a specific characteristic it exhibits then it is all very useful stuff. Names that are obscure in origin or commemorate some long-dead person are of little use to us if we wish to grow something, although the incidental information about some of these names often makes fascinating reading.

Because a botanical name usually consists of only two words, the genus and species, it is obvious that very little information can be incorporated in the name. I for one am not recommending a return to pre-Linnaean systems where a plant may well have had a name that was more like a sentence, but it did at least usually tell you a lot about the subject. Writing labels for plants with their full botanical name must have been a real drag.

I do however object to the tautology that some taxonomists are guilty of. Why repeat the same information in a name when you have the opportunity to say two or more different things about a plant?

A classic example of this is an unusual shrub from South America (more specifically Chile, Peru, Argentina and the Juan Fernandez Islands) called *Rhaphithamnus spinosus*. Its species name is fairly self-explanatory and means that it's spiny, but in a way so does its generic name. From the Greek, it comes from *rhaphis*, which means 'a needle', and *thamnos*, which means 'shrub'. One of its non-accepted synonyms is *R. cyanocarpus*, which tells us that we have a shrub with sharp needles which produces blue berries, much more satisfactory and informative.

The genus is usually listed as consisting of two species, although one of my references suggests that there may be as many as ten. This is probably of little consequence as *R. spinosus* is the only one likely to be met with in cultivation.

It belongs to the Verbena family, although something less like a garden verbena is hard to imagine. The plant makes a large bushy shrub that is supposed to reach 6 metres (20 ft) in the wild, although it is usually 3 to 4 metres (10 to 13 ft) in cultivation; this is quite big enough for most gardens.

In spring you will get masses of tiny soft blue trumpet flowers throughout the plant, which from a distance gives a misty effect. The individual blooms are about 1cm (1/2 in) long and quite narrow. One could say that it is pretty in bloom though subtle.

Its flowers are followed by quite large rich blue berries that I alluded to earlier. These are actually much showier than the flowers.

The foliage is very dark green, glossy and rounded, rather like the common myrtle but even shinier. It is apparently call Prickly Myrtle, and though the two are not related the name does make sense visually.

Considering its impressive armoury, I would hate to tangle with large drifts of it in the wild. Each set of opposite leaves is accompanied by two or three very sharp straight thorns up to 4 cm (1 1/2 in) long so don't bend down to weed with one directly behind you. It will definitely bring you up sharply.

I have found it to be a very good deep green hedge which after four years has made a solid mass about 2 metres (6 ft) tall. The only drawback is that you must be thorough when cleaning up unless you enjoy being impaled later by dry thorny bits when you are weeding.

Most of the time, unless you are hedging *Rhaphithamnus*, you will not need to come in contact with it. Perhaps I should suggest that it might be planted by a window to repel burglars.

William Lobb has never been properly thanked by the gardening fraternity for his introduction of this plant around 1843, and probably never will be.

Rhododendron prinophyllum

When I look back over my own fads and fashions (I mean plants and not platform shoes and body shirts), it surprises me how much I have changed and how often I have changed back.

I can remember as a small child walking through our local hall at flower show time and how I was impressed by gargantuan gladiolus, huge hydrangeas and dinner plate dahlias. The size and colour of these hybrid horrors thrilled and excited me to such an extent that I was moved to grow them. In my innocence I thought them to be the supreme horticultural triumphs.

The same could be said for hybrid rhododendrons. In my teen years with the help and collusion of my father we collected about three hundred different types, many of which had flowers bigger than a champion cabbage.

As I got older most of these plants lost their hold on me and I turned to the charm and elegance of dainty wild species plants. I got carried away by tiny bulbs (some so small you would need thousands to make any show at all). Somehow nature seems to have a balance and sense of rightness that we mere mortals can't hope to duplicate, although not all her triumphs are good garden plants.

This change of direction led to two common misconceptions. The first was that there weren't any worthy plants in any of these genera. No dainty dahlias, graceful gladiolus or refined rhododendrons. The second that there was something wrong with a splash of bright colour, a bit of honest vulgarity and a sense of childlike fun in the garden.

I could now no longer live without a collection of species and early hybrid gladiolus, so elegant and pickable. Nor would my garden be complete without lacecap and oak-leafed hydrangeas.

Even dahlias have found a permanent home with me. I get a great deal of juvenile pleasure from the giant *Dahlia imperialis* and its slightly smaller cousin *D. excelsa* as well as the lovely bronze-leafed hybrids 'Bishop of Llandaff' and 'Yellow Hammer' with their simple single flowers, bright scarlet red in the first and rich yellow in the second.

Most of us are aware that in the huge genus *Rhododendron* with its more than eight hundred species and countless hybrids there are innumerable graceful and desirable plants. It does however still surprise me how often I hear people with supposed taste and knowledge in horticulture dismiss the lot as coarse and vulgar.

It seems silly (even to me) to select just one to discuss here, so I will state from the outset that *Rhododendron prinophyllum* is but one of its group that I must have in my garden. This charming deciduous species from southern Quebec to Virginia was first named *R. roseum*, a simple and appropriate name. This was later changed by W.J. Bean to its current one, and I notice that is also sometimes listed as *R. austrinum*.

It was possibly introduced into England prior to 1812 and received an Award of Merit in 1955 (the year of my birth, a vintage one indeed).

Like most rhodies this one resents drought and heat and likes an acid compost-enriched soil. However unlike most others it will actually grow in quite damp soils and it is found at the edges of sphagnum bogs and in swampy woods throughout its natural habitat.

Expect it to reach about 2 metres (6 ft) tall and to have a lovely informal layered appearance. As its soft grey-green leaves are just breaking through the buds it will open soft pink flowers. These have elegant pointed petals and a wonderful perfume reminiscent of clove-scented carnations. Throughout

summer its form and foliage is light and airy and in autumn the leaves will turn soft yellow and russet before shedding.

It is something of a relief that this enormous genus hasn't accumulated a mass of common names; even rank amateurs seem to have no problem saying or remembering *Rhododendron*.

The name, by the way, comes from the Greek *rhodon*, which means 'rose', and *dendron*, 'tree'. I don't really know if it was named because its flowers were thought to look like roses (which they don't) or because many of them come in shades of pink.

Rhus glabra 'Laciniata'

How often do I hear people asking 'How tall will it grow?'.

It is an obvious and important question, after all you don't want a giant redwood in a tiny suburban garden. It is interesting that other equally important questions aren't asked by many home gardeners. I rarely get asked how long it takes to reach a given height. Even a very small garden could cope with a Huon pine (*Lagarostrobus franklinii*) as not many of us are likely to be around in a few hundred years when it reaches maturity.

Another aspect often forgotten is how wide a particular plant is likely to grow. I have had customers decide against a tall-growing tree with a narrow habit in favour of such things as horizontal or weeping elms. They know the height will be to some extent limited by how tall the tree is grafted, but forget that the spread could easily take up all their front garden as well as their next door neighbour's, to say nothing of those large questing roots and the tendency to sucker if roots are damaged.

I often get asked if a plant can be cut back to restrain its size, but with some plants this will only invigorate it and encourage extra strong growth so that pruning must be done regularly if it is to be successful.

This leads to the topic of manipulating plants to fit a required aspect. We all know about pruning fruit trees and roses to obtain a desired habit and many Australian gardeners are now espaliering trees along walls and fences. Fuchsias and azaleas are being trained as formal standards but few people, in this country at least, are using the age-old techniques of pollarding and coppicing.

For those who don't know, both techniques consist of removing all the current season's growth back to a given point each year, leaving just a small stub of year-old wood with a few buds that will reshoot in spring. In coppicing this is done close to the ground and in pollarding a trunk is established at the desired height first, so it is really coppicing on a standard.

This system is particularly appropriate for plants that have coloured canes in winter. Many willows will pollard or coppice very well and coppicing coloured-stemmed dogwoods such as *Cornus alba* 'Sibirica' will create a lovely effect. All winter these willows and dogwoods will appear like clusters of red, yellow or orange fishing rods that will reflect the winter sun.

Many trees that have large bold leaves, like catalpas or paulownias, will produce enormous foliage if coppiced, giving a wonderful tropical effect to a border and keeping the plants to a moderate size. Of course they won't flower if treated in this way, but after all it isn't flowers that we want when we use these trees as border plants.

Another plant that makes a spectacular foliage effect if coppiced is *Rhus glabra* 'Laciniata', the cut-leafed form of smooth sumach, from North America.

When Rhus is mentioned to Australian gardeners they usually think of that brilliantly autumn-coloured small tree *R. succedanea*, from Asia. Many people are horribly allergic to this plant and it is much debated whether we should grow it or not. I might add that it is now appropriately and more correctly called *Toxicodendron succedaneum* and that *R. glabra* and the related *R. typhina* are generally considered benign.

If left to its own devices *R. glabra* 'Laciniata' will grow into a large shrub of 3 metres (10 ft) or more and its lovely foliage will turn brilliant shades of yellow, orange and scarlet in autumn.

It has a slightly suckering habit that I for one see as a benefit not a drawback, after all what simpler way is there to get more free plants, something of a nurseryman's dream as long as not too many home gardeners take

advantage of it.

This plant can become a truly dramatic garden feature if it is coppiced every winter. It will then produce strong stems rarely more than 1.5 metres (5 ft) tall and its soft ferny leaves can then be expected to grow up to 1 metre (3 ft) long.

When underplanted with big plate-like leaves, perhaps bergenias, and surrounded by tall ornamental grasses like *Miscanthus* a really exotic and impressive effect is assured.

Though this plant gained a First Class Certificate as long ago as 1867, and a more recent Award of Garden Merit in 1984, it is not yet readily available in Australia and with the bad reputation of some of its relatives may never get the popularity it deserves.

It will cope with poor soil although a fertile one will encourage larger leaves. Give it a sunny aspect with good drainage and apart from pruning you can sit back and wait for the compliments to come your way.

Rubus lineatus

If you were to visit my nursery looking for a shrub that was hardy and had really beautiful foliage and I suggested a blackberry, what reaction would I get?

Assuming you didn't just leave, I suppose I could expect some harsh words or if you were of a kindly disposition you might well say 'Now there, dear, you have obviously been overworked. Perhaps you need a holiday or a nice rest in a good sanatorium, you'll soon get used to the straitjacket'.

I hope that I am a good enough salesman to convince you by the end of this profile to try this very superior blackberry, although I won't offer a set of free steak knives or an album of my greatest hits.

The genus *Rubus*, known to all and sundry as blackberries (although it includes raspberries and many other tasty plants), consists of about three hundred species, with perhaps a thousand or more microspecies contributed by the infamous blackberry and its American allies. Obviously they aren't all weeds and out of so many a few must be worth some space in the garden.

The particular species that I hope to sell you is *Rubus lineatus*, which grows wild in such romantic places as the Himalayas, south-western China, Malaysia and Java. It is classed as the supreme foliage plant in the genus by such luminaries as W.J. Bean in his encyclopaedic work *Trees and Shrubs Hardy in the British Isles*.

I'm sure if I didn't tell you it was a black-berry I would have no trouble convincing you to take one home. The impressive leaves are usually divided into five leaflets with up to fifty sets of indented veins, giving it an almost pleated look. They have an arrangement similar to that of a horse chestnut and although they aren't as big they have much more pizazz. This doesn't mean that they are tiny, the central leaflet on a vigorous well-grown plant can be up to 20 cm (8 in) long and 2.5 cm (1 in) wide, which should give you some idea of scale.

Your pleasure needn't stop with the top of the leaves; turn one over and look at the back, it has a wonderful mercurial appearance. It is silky to the touch, silvery in colour and adds much to the overall charm of the plant.

The stems on young growth also have this lovely silvery effect and you may well be pleased to know that they have very few prickles and even these aren't all that sharp.

Its growth habit is quite elegant as it produces tall slightly arching canes that set the leaves off to perfection. These canes can exceed 3 metres (10 ft) and give the plant an almost bamboo quality.

There is a down side to *R. lineatus*, as I'm sure you would expect with even the most elegant blackberry, and that is its suckering habit. Truant canes can pop up well away from the original clump and could be considered something of a nuisance to those of you who like to have plants that stay where they were put. They aren't usually too difficult to deal with unless they come up through the middle of something else and they are a good way to propagate more if you want them. You may even like to give them away to close friends, as long as you warn them so they don't become enemies. Many roses, particularly rugosas, have the same suckering tendencies and I haven't heard of anyone dismissing them because of it. Roses after all are only the rich man's blackberries. Now that I have insulted all the rosarians out there I must point out that *R. lineatus* suckers seem a lot easier to extract than those of a rugosa. If you don't feel your garden would suit a thicket of *Rubus* canes you could opt for growing it in a tub, where it would make a most elegant feature.

If your garden is large and you have an extra area that you wish to develop as a jungle then *R. lineatus* is a most useful addition. This might even make a good spot to go big game hunting with a friendly rajah, just keep your eyes peeled for marauding tigers.

Of course its leaves are its crowning glory but it should also produce classical white blackberry flowers, followed by small red or yellow fruit that the children amongst us may like to pick and eat. I doubt that it will sustain our hungry tiger for long.

Like all self-respecting blackberries it will grow in most soils and aspects but its leaves are better in semi-shade and apart from dealing with its suckers it pays to completely remove some of its oldest canes every so often.

Salix melanostachys

Wet soggy soil isn't perhaps as common as dry parched areas in this country. Nevertheless many gardens include a poorly drained spot, and on larger properties there may be a dam or a lake in the garden. Or dare I mention those wet smelly patches at the end of the septic line in non-sewered country gardens?

Whatever the reason for the bog at the bottom of the garden, most gardeners seem to be at a loss to know what to plant in such a position.

Of course, in larger gardens with plenty of room one may opt for weeping willows, alders, clumps of pampas grass, or the monstrous foliage of the giant Chilean rhubarb (*Gunnera manicata*).

However, you may not have the room to cope with the roots of weeping willows or alders (and they will soon clog the pipes in your septic line anyway), or you may be looking for something a little bit different.

The plant I would like to promote for your soggy bog is *Salix melanostachys*, which originated in Japan and is believed by some authorities to be of hybrid origin, although current thinking suggests that it is a male clone of *S. gracilistyla*. This may well be true.

As the species name of this willow suggests, it produces velvet-like black catkins on its bare stems in late winter, which makes it a most arresting if somewhat strange-looking plant. As the catkins mature they will explode with a mass of soft lemon stamens, tipped with red.

Like all willows it will cope with very wet soil – you could probably grow it in a glass of water. But unlike many of the better-known species it will only grow into a large shrub of about 3 metres (10 ft), and about as wide. The root system is appropriate to the size of the plant and should not create any problems even in quite small gardens.

Pruning, if necessary, could most easily be done by picking sprays of catkins for the house as it lasts well as a cut flower, and I am sure that florists will see the possibilities of this remarkable plant.

The foliage is also attractive, as it is very glossy and an interesting shade of mid green.

When selecting a site to show *S. melanostachys* at its best it is advisable to have a light background, such as the winter sky or a white wall; this will show off the catkins.

I hope that I have convinced you to try this remarkably hardy and quick-growing shrub in your patch of primeval ooze!

Sambucus racemosa 'Plumosa Aurea'

When someone mentions elderberries gardeners will visualise a hardy unexciting deciduous shrub with flat clusters of small white flowers followed by bunches of shiny black berries. Gastronomes may well remember the delights of elderflower fritters, elderflower champagne or elderberry wine. This beverage, for those that haven't tried it, may well bring back memories of old movies with even older ladies living in houses with big cellars stocked with elderberry wine spiked with arsenic.

Sambucus, as the elders are known botanically, is the old Latin name for this group of deciduous shrubs and perennial herbs. There are some twenty or so species, few of which deserve garden space unless you are making fritters, champagne or wine. Remember not to make too much of the first two or you won't have enough berries to make the third.

The common elder, *S. nigra*, is the species that is used for wine making and cooking, and it has produced a range of cultivars with more to offer the eye than the wild form. Some have variegated or gold foliage, some purple. There are yellow-fruited ones and cut-leafed ones, even one with double flowers, which presumably doesn't fruit.

It is however to *Sambucus racemosa*, Red-berried Elder, that the highest accolades must go for a coloured-foliage cultivar.

This shrub, native to continental Europe from Belgium and Spain to Siberia, produced a golden form called *S. racemosa* 'Plumosa Aurea'. It was first sold by Messrs Wezelenburg in 1895 and given its first Award of Merit in that year, followed by another in 1956 and an Award of Garden Merit in 1984. It probably deserves two Awards of Merit but one wonders why they gave the same award to the same shrub twice.

Before I go on singing its praises I must point out that the red-berried elder isn't edible so it won't make red wine. I haven't been able to ascertain if the flowers are fritterable, I hope someone will try it for me and let me know.

Our golden-leafed red-berried elder is described in *The Hillier Manual of Trees and Shrubs* as 'One of the elite of golden foliage shrubs'. I can do nothing more than agree.

It is quite hardy and will tolerate most soil types. It doesn't mind what aspect it faces, although excessive sun may scorch it and dense shade turn it greenish.

Reference books tend to differ about this plant's ability to hold its colour through the season. Mine looses a little colour by mid summer but I don't know if I could cope with its vibrant spring gold all season. I think that how well its colour holds is dependent on aspect and pruning or lack of.

It can grow to 2 metres (6 ft) or more tall although it is usually less if regularly pruned. By cutting out the oldest canes every year or so you will invigorate the plant and it will repay you with extra large and colourful leaves. If you forget to do this for a few years, coppice the whole thing down and all will be forgiven. After pruning, which is usually done in winter, insert your prunings into the ground and hey presto! more golden elders.

In early spring, when it is in vigorous growth, its glorious golden leaves are stained copper. The individual leaflets are prettily serrated, giving a ferny look. As the season progresses the colour changes slightly, as I have already mentioned, but it is always good.

The flowers are in domed clusters and also yellow, so they don't make much impact from a distance.

As yet I have seen no red berries nor do any of my references mention them. I fear that

this superb shrub may have decided not to overdo it, although I wish it would. Perhaps some kind reader has accomplished this feat and will let me know. If on the other hand it is sterile, leave me to hope on regardless. The thought of clusters of brilliant red berries amongst this cheery golden foliage would indeed be a sight.

Sarcococca ruscifolia

In nearly every garden there is a dry shaded spot. It may be a south-facing wall under the eaves or under the canopy of large trees with strong moisture-seeking roots everywhere.

It can be a big problem to find quality plants for such a position and as long as you are not looking for something with a bright splash of colour and are content with a shrub of quiet charm and elegance then you may decide on *Sarcococca ruscifolia*, from China.

The generic name comes from the Greek *sarkos*, meaning 'flesh', and *kokkos*, 'a berry', which makes this strange name descriptive.

In England it is known as Christmas Box, as it flowers and fruits in winter and looks like the box bush we use for hedging, and it is nice to know that it is also related to box. Both genera belong to the Box family, Buxaceae.

As the photograph shows, its rich red berries are quite large and showy. However, you will have to look closely to see the tiny green-white flowers. These blooms do have a lovely fragrance that more than makes up for their lack of size.

The shrub will grow to rather less than 2 metres (6 ft), and although it can be trimmed or cut its natural arching habit is one of its major assets. The foliage and berries last well in a vase but I cut only an odd limb or two for the house so as not to ruin its shape.

Although not fussy about soil, and equally happy in acid or alkaline conditions as well as being able to cope with quite dry conditions, to get the best from it the soil should be well cultivated and humus added to give it a good start. Keep up the watering for the first summer or so until its roots are well established. Once it is under way it is an easy plant for the shady spot.

Like so many plants from China, *S. ruscifolia* was introduced by E.H. Wilson, in 1901. It received an Award of Merit only seven years later.

Although there are some fourteen species in the genus few are grown and available to Australian gardeners. There is, however, one other that I have. *S. confusa* will grow in the same way as *S. ruscifolia* but it is smaller and rarely exceeds 60 cm (24 in). Its berries are jet black instead of red.

Sarcococca confusa is appropriately enough of uncertain origin, although probably it is also from China. It has been in cultivation in the West since about 1916 and received an Award of Garden Merit in 1984 and an Award of Merit in 1989. Not bad for a mixed-up little thing.

Sasa veitchii

Suggest bamboo to the average gardener and you might as well be offering a virulent strain of bubonic plague. The reaction is usually much the same. All those questing rhizomes ready to engulf the flowerbeds and create neighbourly disquiet when they stealthily go under the fence!

This is certainly true of some of the running species but even these can be controlled if proper precautions are taken. You could try laying down an impenetrable barrier to curb their invasive tendencies or you could use them as a lawn specimen in an island bed so that wayward shoots could be promptly dealt with using the lawnmower.

It must also be remembered that most species have a comparatively short active period and if you get out there with a sharp spade (or perhaps a back hoe for the larger ones) and deal with the runners at the right time you can then take a rest until next year.

Keep in mind that this group of giant grasses, for this is indeed what they are, encompasses some ninety genera with perhaps one thousand species and they can't all be unruly thugs. Many species are more likely to go for a quiet stroll instead of jogging through the garden and so are much better behaved. There are also many clumping species that will be almost sedentary so these may well be the best for the more timid gardeners amongst you.

You might well say why bother with bamboos at all? After all, there are so many other useful garden plants we can be growing.

The Chinese and Japanese gardeners, and painters for that matter, have long appreciated the charms of bamboo, which has subtle and sometimes not so subtle elegance and character that few other plants can mimic.

Now let us get a bit more specific and discuss just one of the many bamboos that I wouldn't be without.

Sasa veitchii is a running bamboo that will make a lovely tall weed-suppressing groundcover as long as you don't think that it is the weed. It can grow into a thicket about 1 metre (3 ft) tall and as wide as you let it, so in smaller gardens it may be better to keep it in a pot.

It will grow well under large deciduous trees, where it will be somewhat more restrained due to the drier soil and root competition, and its marvellous parchment-edged leaves will give good colour in darkish corners. This isn't variegation at all but the dead edges of the leaves and it is most obvious in autumn and winter. In his *Manual of Cultivated Broad-Leaved Trees and Shrubs* Gerd Krüssmann suggests that the very thing that makes this bamboo beautiful for me is 'of little ornamental value because of the unattractive dry leaf margins'.

To keep *S. veitchii* neat it is a good idea to cut it right down every second year at the end of winter, just before the new growth starts. This could even be accomplished with a lawnmower, if it's powerful enough, or a slasher. Unless you have a huge patch, secateurs are usually preferred.

In its native Japan it is known as Kuma-zasa and its botanical name is a corruption from this.

The famous names connected with this plant are quite impressive. It was introduced in 1880 by Charles Maries (1851-1902) and was named after and collected for the well-known nursery of James Veitch and Sons, originally of Exeter and later of Chelsea, the leading nurserymen of their day. They sent collectors all over the world, and trained numbers of the best gardeners.

It received an Award of Merit in 1898, when its invasive nature wasn't perhaps realised and when bamboos were the height of fashion.

I suppose I should give another British horticulturist the penultimate say, just as a warning. W.J. Bean in his huge work, *Trees and Shrubs Hardy in the British Isles*, isn't enthusiastic about *S. veitchii*. He says, 'This species is too invasive and shabby looking to be admitted into the garden, and does nothing to beautify woodland, where it will in time form vast thickets, difficult to eradicate'.

I will however have the ultimate say and at the risk of going against the verdicts of such luminaries as Bean and Krüssman would like to modestly suggest that the foliage of *S. veitchii* is charming and if you think ahead before you plant I'm sure you too will enjoy the experience.

Schima wallichii

Why are there so few good summer-flowering trees in parks and gardens? It is after all the time of year that most of us have the inclination to be out doors enjoying the fruits of our garden labour. The days are long and warm, the barbecue is working hard and we should all be trying to add colour and interest to our gardens at this time.

I know that there isn't any lack of smaller flowering plants. Many shrubs and perennials are at their peak but I like to be able to look up at flowers as well as down. There certainly are many lovely summer trees. My theory for their non-appearance is that most gardeners buy what they see in flower and it is in spring that nursery visiting is at its peak, when we are all frantic to see our gardens full of colour after the spartan winter months. By summer we are usually too busy watering and caring for our existing plants to be interested in buying more.

Another factor peculiar to flowering trees is that few of them flower at a small size, so even if they are available you aren't likely to see them flowering at a size that you could buy. Most nursery staff like plants that sell themselves as it is very time consuming having to wax lyrical about a plant to convince a prospective purchaser.

I can understand people not wishing to plant some unknown tree on someone else's recommendation, although I might add that it has never stopped me! I find it exciting to experiment and some of my now-favourite plants came into my possession this way. Occasionally they have turned out to be nothing but a yawn. This doesn't however deter me as I look on gaps created by removals as a new opportunity.

One summer-flowering tree that has the added disadvantage of not being hardy in England, where most of the gardening books we southern gardeners use come from, is *Schima wallichii*. It belongs to the Tea family (Theaceae), with the far better-known camellias. Depending on which taxonomist you follow it is either monotypic (consisting of one species) with a broad distribution through India eastwards to Taiwan and south to Indonesia or it consists of up to fifteen closely related species. If you accept it as one species you will find some difference in the shape, size and colour of foliage as well as flower size. This doesn't really matter as the differences visually are slight although there will undoubtedly be some difference in hardiness depending on the provenance of the material.

Now we should get down to some specifics. *S. wallichii* will make a small to medium evergreen tree with a dense bushy head, up to about 8 metres (26 ft) or so although wild specimens have been recorded at 40 metres (130 ft). I assume that if it ever reaches these lofty heights in cultivation it will be someone else's problem.

Its large leathery deep green leaves are always attractive but particularly so in spring when the new leaves are a lovely shade of bronze-red. The flowers, which will normally be produced only on plants that have been in residence for a few years, are about 5 cm (2 in) across. Not suprisingly, they are shaped like single camellias with a boss of yellow stamens. Why you would plant one instead of a camellia is due to the fact that it blooms in late summer and has a pleasant if not strong fragrance.

Any aspect that suits its famous cousin should be ideal for *Schima*. It likes a little shelter from hot sun and winds, a humus-rich lime-free soil and enough space to show itself off.

It can be propagated from cuttings or seed if available, although I suspect that seedlings may take considerably longer to start flowering.

The origin of the genetic name is obscure. One of my references suggests that it may be from the Greek work skiasma, which means 'shadow' or 'shelter', referring to the thick leafy crown of the tree. *The New Royal Horticultural Society Dictionary of Gardening* suggests that it comes from Arabic but gives no further information and as the tree isn't native to this region one wonders what the connection is.

The species name isn't obscure and commemorates Nathaniel Wallich (1786-1854), who had problems with his own name as he was originally called Nathan Wolff. He was a Danish botanist who went to India as a surgeon at Serampore, near Calcutta, and later became Superintendent of the Calcutta Botanic Garden from 1814 until 1841.

Sequoiadendron giganteum 'Pendulum'

Some plants are so bizarre in shape and form that it would take a brave gardener to plant them.

One such plant is *Sequoiadendron giganteum* 'Pendulum', the weeping form of the Californian Big Tree, also known as the Mammoth Tree or Wellingtonia. This last name is actually a long defunct name for the genus.

The non-pendulous form is one of the world's most massive living things so it is obviously not a tree that you would plant unless your garden is something of a grand estate.

In California the largest specimens have been given names and the General Sherman Tree is reportedly the biggest. It measures some 84 metres (275 feet) in height with a girth of 25 metres (80 feet) at 1.4 metres (4 ft 6 in) from the ground. The trunk volume is some 1,400 cubic metres (49,440 cubic ft) and it has an estimated weight of 2,500 tonnes.

The oldest authenticated age comes from a tree that was felled and was some 3,200 years old. It must have taken quite a long time to count the rings and wouldn't it be awful if you lost count halfway through. I hope the people involved felt it was worth killing the tree to find out that it was 3,200 years old.

The strange name Sequoiadendron with its superabundance of vowels has an interesting origin. *Dendron* of course means 'tree', something of an understatement I would suggest. Sequoia, who lived from 1770 to 1843, was the son of a German-American father and a Cherokee mother. He was bought up by the tribe and though he knew no English he later invented the Cherokee alphabet. The adoption of this syllabary by the Cherokees in 1821 quickly made a good percentage of the tribe literate. This didn't however stop the greedy whites from stealing their territory and killing some four thousand of their tribe. The word *Sequoia* actually means 'opossum' and was used as a nickname for people of mixed blood. The Sequoia of our story was also known as George Gist but as far as I know no taxonomist has suggested changing the name of the tree to Gistodendron, which is a relief.

Now to get back to our weeping form. *S. giganteum* 'Pendulum' was discovered in Nantes in 1863 and received a First Class Certificate in 1882. One wonders if it would be selected for such a high honour these days, as gardeners of discernment and taste don't have the same sense of fun and enjoyment of the bizarre that our Victorian counterparts had.

It can assume fantastic shapes but is usually a narrow waving column with branches that hang straight down the trunk. The specimen in the photograph is growing in my nursery garden; its strange stepped appearance is due to the pruning techniques of the sulphur-crested cockatoos. Each time they nip its tip out a side branch then has to curve around to become a leader. It is certainly an odd-looking thing, but what a great conversation piece.

Hardly a customer enters my domain that doesn't ask what that strange tree is. Children are particularly smitten with it. *S. giganteum* 'Pendulum' must have the greatest height for width ratio of any tree. The largest specimen in Britain is a stunning 32 metres by 2.5 metres (105 ft by 8 ft) in 1984 and is growing in the well-known Welsh garden of Bodnant.

I have probably now put you all off planting one but do remember we will all be dead well before this tree becomes a giant; also, the width that something spreads is far more important than its height as long as you haven't planted it directly below wires or the eaves of the house.

Another bonus in planting this tree is that visitors when being given directions to your house can just be told to look out for the shaggy digit pointing irreverently skywards. If

you do decide to plant one, and I hope some of you will, don't be put off by price. Like many other conifers this one is usually grafted, which is a bit time consuming, and although it has a reasonable growth rate when it has got going, about 30 cm (12 in) a year in its formative years, it will grow quite slowly and take a little while to realise that it wants to be a tree.

Anyway we wouldn't want it to be cheap, then everyone might plant one and it would be most disconcerting to see suburbs full of these coniferous conversation pieces.

You will be pleased to know that your initial investment isn't likely to be at risk as this tree is remarkably hardy and free of any major pests or diseases (except for cockatoos). It isn't fussy about soil type and any reasonably well-drained but not too dry aspect will do.

Sorbaria aitchisonii

The accompanying photo almost speaks for itself! A plant like *Sorbaria aitchisonii* is obviously very elegant and desirable. So why haven't we all got it?

S. aitchisonii is a hardy deciduous shrub to about 3 metres (10 ft), native to Afghanistan, Pakistan and Kashmir. It has been in cultivation since 1880.

This species is, in my opinion, the best of its tribe even though all members of this small genus have a strong family resemblance.

My reasons are that it has reddish-coloured petioles that set off its fine pale green foliage very well, and when the flowers have finished its seed heads are at least for some time a lovely deep burgundy, making it valuable in the garden even after flowering.

At one time all the species were included in the *Spiraea* genus; they were separated into their own due mainly to their compound leaves.

All the species are summer-flowering and in the case of *S. aitchisonii* the panicles can be up to 30 cm (12 in) long. Both the flowers and the seed heads (particularly the latter) are good for cutting and last well in a vase.

It isn't at all fussy about soil or aspect but is normally more floriferous when grown in a sunny position.

A well-grown specimen can reach 3 metres tall (10 ft) and if allowed to sucker (no-one says you have to) it could be equally wide.

If it has any vices it may be this slightly suckering habit, although this is a good way to obtain more plants. It can also be propagated from hardwood cuttings rowed out in the open ground during winter.

Pruning consists of cutting out completely any old, exhausted wood every so often. As the flowers are produced on the current season's wood the plant can be pruned quite hard in winter. This is the best time to prune, as you can see what your are doing. When the seed heads are no longer ornamental, wood that has flowered should be cut back to some fat buds.

I find the plant useful behind herbaceous perennials and heritage roses as it makes a soft background that doesn't dominate the foreground plants but is bushy enough to block in the view during the growing season.

Finally, like so many plants in this book, disputes over names exist. The genus name obviously means that this plant resembles *Sorbus*, the rowan or mountain ash; both genera belong to the Rose family, Rosaceae. The species name commemorates Dr James Aitchison, a British physician and botanist who discovered it in the Kurram Valley, Afghanistan, in 1879. This is the name used in *The Hillier Manual of Trees and Shrubs* and also by W.J. Bean in his *Trees and Shrubs Hardy in the British Isles*.

Other equally eminent authorities prefer *S. tomentosa* var. *angustifolia* or *S. angustifolia* as a synonym for *Sorbus aitchisonii*. Take your pick, one of them is correct if only until the botanists invent another name.

Stachyurus chinensis 'Magpie'

Winter-flowering shrubs are always welcome in the garden as well as useful to cut and take indoors when the weather is too inclement for long walks around your estate.

My only reservation is that many of them have nothing further to give you and so will make no impact during summer when the garden is most utilised and should be at its best.

I couldn't live without a large plant of *Chimonanthus praecox*, the much loved winter sweet, for it has the most sumptuous perfume of all winter plants but it must be admitted that it is quite second-rate the rest of the year.

My plant of *Chimonanthus* is right next to my front step where it can intoxicate as I pass throughout late winter. In such a prime spot it is sad to have something that is a bore for much of the year and I have overcome this to an extent by using it as a host for a vigorous large-flowered clematis called 'Twilight'. The clematis is cut to the socks each winter so that it doesn't hide the winter sweet and from mid summer till late autumn I have a mass of large mauve flowers to keep me excited.

One winter-flowered shrub that will offer year-round interest, although unfortunately no noticeable perfume so it can't take the place of winter sweet, is *Stachyurus chinensis* 'Magpie'. The genus is a small Asian one of up to ten species but only the above mentioned *S. chinensis* 'Magpie' and S. praecox are likely to be met with, albeit too infrequently in Australian gardens.

In my climate I find that *S. praecox,* which is commonly called early spiketail, often holds foliage through the winter, thus lessening the impact of its flowers. In warmer summer climates it tends to stop growing earlier and sheds properly.

This is never a problem with *S. chinenses* 'Magpie', which was discovered at Hillier's Nursery in England about 1945 and differs from the species because it has variegated foliage.

I will now take you through a year in the life of this shrub which will hopefully convince you of its merits.

Its flower spikes are matured on the plant during autumn so that when its leaves shed the branches support strange deep bronze-red drooping spikes. These buds are interesting if not showy and will keep you amused until late winter, when they produce their lovely little pale greenish-yellow cup-shaped flowers. The photograph shows them attractively set off with a sprinkling of snow, something no lowland Australian gardener is likely to duplicate.

The flowers are lovely as cut material for the house but as its spikes are stiff they tend to stick out in odd directions if you can't arrange them at the same angle as they were on the bush. To give you some idea of scale, the flower spikes are usually about 8 to 10 cm (3 to 4 in) long.

From spring till autumn you will have its large variegated leaves to keep you happy. These are about 15 cm (6 in) long and 6 cm ($2^1/2$ in) wide with a long tapering tip. The base colour is a greyish-green with an irregular cream to lemon edge often tinged deep pink and with reddish veins. Having written this it all sounds rather hectic. The effect is in fact fairly soft and subtle for a variegated shrub although it can be somewhat unstable and often throws branches with pure white leaves. These are of no use to the plant as they contain no green pigment but they are nice in a vase.

As autumn arrives the leaves will turn soft yellows, mellow oranges and dusty burgundies. It isn't perhaps in the top ranking of colourful autumn foliage although my description sounds good. Some years it is definitely better than others and the effect is unusual and pretty rather than spectacular.

If all of the above isn't enough, the shape of the plant should definitely tip the scales. It is a multi-stemmed shrub usually no more than 3 metres (10 ft) tall and often as wide. The branches have a horizontal arrangement with the flowers hanging below, so if you remove the lower branches it will arch over above your head and you can view the flowers better. This will also give more ground space, which can be used to underplant with complementary early bulbs or hellebores, and the branches will not poke you in the eye as you pass by.

Stachyurus isn't fussy about soil although it will do better in one enriched with organic material and it certainly appreciates mulching.

An aspect in semi-shade or sun protected from hot winds should suit. This shouldn't be beyond most of us.

Finally, its strange botanic name comes from the Greek *stachys*, which means 'an ear of corn', hence 'a spike', and *oura*, 'a tail'. Literally 'a spiketail', and its family Stachyuraceae is represented by only this one genus.

Staphylea colchica

I have something of a soft spot for plants that have off-beat and unusual perfumes.

I am not unimpressed by the fabulous perfumes of such well-known plants as roses, lilacs, honeysuckle and similar delights. However the majority of scented flowers smell flowery. Honeysuckle smells like honeysuckle, lilac in most cases smells of lilac and a rose by any other name would smell like whatever its new name was.

When selecting scented plants for my garden I love to find plants that have perfumes that evoke images of quite unrelated things.

Another fun part of such plants is that scents are perceived in quite different ways by different people and it amuses me to see if I agree with them. Be warned, however, because if you are told that something has the smell of a ripe banana or whatever, that is usually just what you will smell.

I used to love the smell of *Osmanthus delavayi* until the day I read somewhere that it smelt of cheap suntan lotion. I think it was 'cheap' that put me off, not the lotion.

The smell of *Azara microphylla* is usually described as vanilla but for me that is only part of it. I think it smells like a freshly-baked chocolate cake, which we all know contains vanilla, and it gets my mouth watering as no rose could.

A plant I have written about before is the Moroccan broom (now botanically called *Argyrocytisus battandieri*, although it is still usually listed as *Cytisus*). Every book says that it smells of pineapple and yet when I suggest that it is more like the fragrance of a ripe green apple no-one has disagreed with me. I haven't even had to raise my voice.

Michelia compressa smells like a mixture of banana and bubble gum and the plant of this profile, *Staphylea colchica*, smells of coconut with perhaps a dash of nutmeg and vanilla. It sounds like a recipe for a coconut rice pudding. Whilst still on its perfume, I have read that it has an orange blossom scent so either I'm way off the track or orange blossom doesn't smell like it used to.

Now let us discuss the other virtues and vices of this much under-used shrub.

It comes from the family Staphyleaceae and belongs to a small genus of about eleven species of hardy deciduous shrubs or small trees.

The most obvious feature of the genus is the curious but decorative seed pods, which also give the genus its common name of Bladdernut.

After its lovely white flowers finish, and these are in evidence during late spring (a most useful flowering season), it will produce quite large two- or three-celled papery bladders in which can be found its hard pea-sized seeds. These bladders start green and turn coppery-brown once ripe.

Both the scented flowers and the seed pods are useful as cut material for a vase, just remember not to pick too much of the former or you'll get little of the latter.

S. colchica will make a tall upright shrub to 4 metres (13 ft). It has that one unforgivable vice, it suckers, but I don't find them difficult to deal with. I have noticed that none of my reference works even mention this habit. If I want to sell it I probably shouldn't either.

Its foliage is pleasant if not exciting and usually consists of three to five light green leaflets that will often turn a soft yellow before they shed. The flower panicles can be up to 13 cm (5^{1}/4 in) long and nearly as wide and its bladders are usually about 8 cm (3 in) long.

The name *Staphylea* was coined by some desperate and unimaginative botanist and comes from the Greek word *staphyle*, which means 'a cluster' and alludes to the highly distinctive fact that the flowers are found in clusters.

Apart from dealing with the aforementioned ;uckers the only thing one needs to do to ›laddernut is enjoy it. You may wish to remove ;ome of its oldest wood after flowering but I loubt that it will make much difference one vay or the other.

It will grow in any sunny or semi-shaded ıspect and any well-drained but not deadly dry soil will be fine. If you decide to reward it with a feed and some tasty mulch you will reap as you have sown.

Finally, it was introduced from the south Caucasus into cultivation in 1850 and was awarded a First Class Certificate in 1879 when exhibited by James Veitch and Sons. It doesn't seem to have had much press since.

Styrax japonica

Small trees that flower in early summer are a great acquisition for any garden. When the last of the cherries and other earlier trees have finished and summer's more sombre greens dominate the treescape something with a spring-like appearance is always a pleasant surprise.

Of all the trees I grow that flower at this desirable time I would have to list *Styrax* japonica up there with the best.

There seems to be quite some dispute over the form of the species name with this plant. W.J. Bean's *Trees and Shrubs Hardy in the British Isles* and *The Hillier Manual of Trees and Shrubs* both spell it *japonica*. Gerd Krüssmann in his *Manual of Cultivated Broad-Leaved Trees and Shrubs* opts for *japonicus* and *The New Royal Horticultural Society Dictionary of Gardening* has decided on *japonicum*. What is a humble gardener supposed to do when confronted with conflicting opinions in such erudite publications?

The name *Styrax* was first used for *S. officinalis*, from which the resin storax is extracted by tapping the bark. This resin was used as incense. Again there seems to be some controversy about this, as some references have suggested that storax is actually tapped from a species of liquidambar and others have maintained that incense storax comes from *Styrax* and medical storax (don't ask me what you would use it for) comes from the liquidambar.

A learned friend tells me that in the original Greek *styrax* has both a masculine and a feminine form. Herodatus uses the feminine form when describing the shrub or tree that yields the gum called storax. This would make *japonica* the correct species name. (Compulsive collectors of trivia may like to know that the masculine form of styrax means 'the spike at the butt end of a spear shaft'.)

All of this is of course completely irrelevant to us as *S. japonica* apparently has nothing to do with resins, medical or otherwise.

I have grown only four of the more than one hundred species in this genus and although I don't think there is a bad one in the whole bunch and wish to make the acquaintance of many more, I feel that surely none could surpass the beauty of *S. japonica*.

For those kind souls that may be moved to send me plants or seeds I will mention that I have so far obtained my selected species plus *S. obassia*, *S. confusa* and *S. odoratissima*. I can't even find a reference to the last two in any of my books but they are lovely anyway.

S. japonica obviously comes from Japan but it is also native to China and Korea; it belongs to the family Styraceae.

It makes a graceful small tree up to about 8 metres ((26 ft) tall and is usually broadly pyramidal in outline but will become more spreading with age, like the rest of us. The branches are arranged in fan-shaped tiers that are normally horizontal or slightly ascending, until gravity has its way and again like many of us things start to droop a bit with maturity.

The leaves are neat and bright green, about 6 cm by 3 cm ($2^1/2$ in by $1^1/4$ in) and in autumn turn a pleasing shade of soft buttery yellow. It also develops attractive bark with age, all of which adds up to a tree of great distinction even without having mentioned its crowning glory, the flowers. These lovely drooping bells are usually pure white (although pink forms are known) and are produced in huge quantities suspended below the limbs. Add the fact that the flowers are slightly scented, not to mention its useful flowering time, and what more could one possibly want? Well believe it or not, the story doesn't end here. As the flowers pass they are followed by quite ornamental pea-sized hard seeds that start life a silvery green and turn brown when ready to drop, which is usually about the time the leaves do.

The seeds of *S. officinalis* were apparently once used to make rosaries and I see no reason why you couldn't start a cottage industry with its Asian cousin. This would of course stop you from raising new plants from the seed. If I haven't put you off trying your hand at propagation perhaps the fact that the seeds usually take two years to germinate might do the trick.

If you want to add this lovely little tree to your garden, it likes a sunny to semi-shaded aspect with shelter from strong and/or hot winds. Make sure the ground is well cultivated with plenty of humus added, this should be well mulched to keep the roots cool. It resents both drought and sodden conditions. Plant it where you can walk underneath the branches, this is the best way to appreciate its flowers.

Finally, *Styrax japonica* was introduced to Kew Botanic Gardens in 1862 by Richard Oldham and received a First Class Certificate in 1885 and an Award of Garden Merit in 1984.

Syringa meyeri 'Palibin'

When you think about lilac (the shrub, not the colour) it will depend on your personality as to how you will react.

Those of us that are romantics will visualise heavy heads of mauve, white or purple flowers like great bunches of grapes, exquisitely scented and just ready to pick in huge bunches for the house. Those of a more practical disposition will say it's all very well planting lilacs but don't forget that their season is usually short, the bushes large and bulky, the foliage dreary, the dead flower heads dreadful and unless they are grafted on to privet they sucker all over the place. Not forgetting that when they are grafted if the privet doesn't shoot below the graft, and it usually does, then the whole thing is likely to be short-lived due to long term incompatibility problems between the stock and the scion.

The true romantics, the ones that will fill their gardens with roses knowing there isn't such a thing as too many roses, or plant masses of evocative-sounding things like honeysuckle or jasmine ignoring the fact that both they and their gardens will probably be engulfed in no time, will say 'I can't live without lilac, I literally swoon when it's in flower – albeit a short swoon'.

Here I must admit to being something of a pragmatist. I haven't found it necessary to plant lilacs (at least the well-known hybrids) in my garden. I can always visit friends who have more space or who don't care if the the lilac bushes are lovely for such a short time. I can then enjoy the sumptuous display and not have to look at them again until next year. If I'm extra lucky I may well be sent home with a good-sized bunch of cut lilac to grace my home as well.

There is however a lilac quite unlike the great big hybrids which I would not deny myself. It is known as *Syringa meyeri* 'Palibin', but it may also (unfortunately) be found listed as *S. palibiniana*, *S. microphylla* 'Minor', *S. velutina* and *S. meyeri* 'Ingwersen's Dwarf'.

S. meyeri itself is something of a mystery, having never been found in the wild. It was introduced from gardens near Beijing by Frank Meyer (1875-1918), a Dutch botanist who was sent to China by the U.S. Department of Agriculture to collect plants of economic importance. (The Meyer lemon is another of his introductions.) Due to this lack of wild material some authorities have suggested that *S. meyeri* may be of hybrid origin. If this does turn out to be correct then we must assume that its dwarf form, 'Palibin', is also of impure heritage.

This lilac is thus far the smallest growing and will take up little room in the garden, a great boon to the space conscious. Even after years of non-pruning you are unlikely to have a plant that will exceed 1.2 metres (4 ft) and it will always be a neat and shapely one at that.

It is often recommended as a rock-garden subject but I would suggest that it would be appropriate in only the largest of these. It would be better as a middle or front of border plant or even perhaps as a low informal hedge.

The clusters of rich mauve, scented flowers probably don't last any longer than the large hybrid types but apart from the already mentioned space-saving stature this plant has other strings to its bow not dreamt of by its vulgar relatives. The foliage instead of being dull and boring is pert and pretty. The individual leaves are rounded and attractively scalloped; they are a fresh pale green at flowering and in autumn turn a quite respectable shade of reddish-bronze.

Although it has a suckering habit it has nothing of the thuggish nature that more usual varieties have. It produces only small numbers and I would suggest that they are

never in quantity enough to meet the demand. Having said all this, I would suggest that grafted plants are pointless and definitely to be avoided if you are offered any.

As with its taller relatives, it is advisable to prune out the spent flower heads to keep a tidy look. Give it a sunny well-drained aspect and a good fertile soil and away you go.

If its foliage isn't enough to excite you for the rest of the season plant some *Viola cornuta* around its feet. This lovely little plant will weave its way up through the lowest branches and produce masses of little soft blue-mauve pansies throughout the summer and autumn.

In Greek legend the nymph Syrinx was pursued by that letch and drunkard, Pan, the god of carousal. It wasn't made clear to me as to how it happened but poor Syrinx was turned into a hollow reed from which Pan made his first flute.

The name *Syringa* thus means 'hollow stem' and these plants were once known as Pipe Tree or Blow Stem, names that have fortunately been left behind in the mists of time.

Finally, *Syringa meyeri* 'Palibin' has received an Award of Merit and an Award of Garden Merit, both of which were bestowed on it in 1984.

Telopea truncata

The genus *Telopea*, better known as the waratah, is a small one consisting of some four species, all restricted to Australia. The most famous and glamorous is *T. speciosissima*, which is from New South Wales and of course is that State's floral emblem.

It can be somewhat difficult if conditions don't suit it and as it is a rather gawky shrub it isn't of much garden merit except when in bloom and then it will be a dominant feature due to the size and rich colour of the flowers.

Breeding in recent times has created some bushy, floriferous and hardier hybrids that are much better garden plants. One such is the rich red 'Shady Lady', as well as some of the newer white-flowered clones.

Although flower size is reduced in the other species this shouldn't deter you from planting them if you can find some.

T. oreades, the Gippsland waratah, is probably the largest-growing species, sometimes exceeding 12 metres (40 ft) in the wild although usually smaller in cultivation. Its flower heads are smaller and flatter than those of *T. speciosissima*, but at 10 cm (4 in) or so across and of a rich crimson will still make an impressive show as well as good cut flowers. The plant has rich green leathery leaves and it is usually a bushy upright plant more serviceable than its more northern counterpart.

By the way, a rare yellow-flowered form is supposed to exist in the gullies of Gippsland and I do hope someone will propagate and release it. I hope it isn't a myth.

If the size of *T. oreades* is daunting we can travel further south to Tasmania, the home of *T. truncata*, predictably called the Tasmanian Waratah.

This species has flowers quite similar to *T. oreades* and of similar size but the plant is usually a medium open shrub up to 2 metres (6 ft) although wild specimens have been recorded at 4 metres (13 ft).

Its open habit isn't gawky and it can be made much bushier by pruning; the best way to prune is to cut the flowers for the house.

A rare yellow form of this species does exist and is in cultivation. At least two clones have been discovered, one of which has been named *T. truncata* 'Essie Huxley' after its finder, a charming lady who is a great Tasmanian plant collector. Her garden is a treasure-trove of native and exotic plants that had me drooling when I visited her a while ago. She kindly gave me cuttings of her waratah but alas! they didn't strike. Perhaps one day she will allow me to try again.

The usually stunning red flowers are produced in summer and it must be one of the most obvious plants in the Tasmanian mountains when in bloom. With its background of silvery blue eucalyptus foliage it is a sight worth seeing.

To grow this plant well, select a well-drained site which is sunny but sheltered from hot winds. An open sandy acidic soil with added leaf-mould should suit well, although soils appropriate for rhododendrons will also be fine. Make sure the roots are shaded or well mulched and don't allow it to dry out. Unlike many of our mainland natives, it isn't at all drought-tolerant.

As with many other plants in the Protea family it should never be fed with strong fertilisers, particularly those high in phosphates; these will usually prove fatal.

T. truncata is the hardiest species in the English climate and its form *T. truncata* 'Essie Huxley' is being grown by Hillier's Nursery, according to their manual. The red form received an Award of Merit in 1934 and even a First Class Certificate in 1938. They obviously appreciate it although this might be

due partially to the fact that they can't grow *Telopea speciosissima*. It does seem to me a pity that we aren't growing it more.

The botanical name *Telopea* comes from the Greek word *telopos*, which appropriately means 'seen from afar', as all of this genus certainly can be.

Trochodendron aralioides

There is something distinctly classy about trees and shrubs that have a layered or tiered habit. They have a strong presence in any garden setting, creating a bold structure amongst the lesser and more ordinary green lumps that tend to predominate.

If your requirements also include bold evergreen foliage and shade tolerance then the list of possible candidates is short indeed. What if you also want a plant that has foliage in a lovely mid green and not that really dark green that most shade-tolerant plants tend to have?

The one plant that I'm sure has sprung to mind with you as it has with me is *Trochodendron aralioides*, from Japan, Taiwan and South Korea. It is a wonderful shade-tolerant evergreen shrub or small tree that is supposed to reach 20 metres (65 ft) in the wild but rarely more than 5 metres (16 ft 6 in) in gardens. Even if it could get to its full height under cultivation it is slow enough growing that none of us will be around to worry about it. My own specimen is about 3 metres (10 ft) tall after ten years in exceptionally good soil and in a more than congenial climate.

The tiered habit of the branches is reinforced by the fact that the leaves tend to be clustered at the top of the twigs in much the same way as those of the better-known rhododendrons. These tiers are never flat but undulate in a most pleasing way, giving structure without formality.

Individually the leaves are quietly beautiful. They are up to 15 cm (6 in) long, thick and leathery, with attractively scalloped margins. They sit almost horizontally, making a charming rosette to surround the strangely attractive flowers.

Although the individual blooms are small, green and lacking petals or sepals they are of such an interesting shape and held in nice upright spikes that they are an attractive feature. When available they are often used for flower arranging. The flowers consist of a hemispherical disc edged with numerous stamens, something like a catherine wheel. In fact the name *Trochodendron* literally translates as 'wheel tree'.

It blooms in late spring and into early summer but may take some years to start flowering freely. Don't feel that you are too impatient to wait, just remember that it is really as a foliage shrub that you would plant it in the first place.

Something that I have never seen mentioned in a book anywhere (until now) is that *Trochodendron* has lovely growth buds. These are quite long and tapered and enclosed in pretty pale green bracts stained with salmon pink. They are attractive throughout winter and spring until the leaves explode.

Although *Trochodendron* can be grown in a reasonably sunny site its leaves can bleach a bit, turning it a sickly yellow green instead of the rich apple green it should be. So give it a cool shady corner with adequate space to allow it to show itself off properly and all should be well.

It doesn't seem to have any preference when it comes to soil and will even tolerate some dryness once established. You will however be amply rewarded for any small services you wish to provide, like adequate water and occasional manuring.

Botanists have been debating this plant's botanical position for as long as it has been in Western cultivation, which happened some time just prior to its first flowering for James Veitch and Sons' nursery in 1894.

It is thought to be quite primitive and its wood closely resembles that of conifers, which of course predate flowering angiosperms, of which it is one. Now most authorities place it

in the monotypic family Trochodendraceae, which with Tetracentraceae constitutes the order Trochodendrales. I bet you are all so pleased to know all that!

Trochodendron has aromatic bark, which is something you don't want to test too often if the tree's health means anything to you. It is apparently regularly epiphytic in the wild, usually found growing in Japanese cedars (*Cryptomeria japonica*). Apart from those facts, there is little else to be said about this attractive botanical oddity, except to mention in passing that it received an Award of Merit in 1976.

Ulmus parvifolia 'Frosty'

How many times have I been asked for the perfect tree for a small garden? Goodness only knows.

What most customers want is something that is very hardy, meaning that it will grow in rock- hard clay, survive without watering in summer and waterlogging in winter. It has to stand blazing sun, strong winds and the regular attentions of the dog.

It must of course grow very fast and yet not grow too large, 5 to 6 metres (16 ft to 20 ft) seems quite tall to some gardeners even for their major specimen tree. The shape must be elegant and it must give 'colour' (green isn't a colour apparently) in the garden for as long as possible, all year round if it could be arranged. Naturally it must have a well-behaved root system that won't damage the foundations or the concrete path. Those of a tidy disposition usually demand that the tree isn't messy, after all we don't want to have to rake up after it if we can help it.

Probably the only thing that could possibly meet all of these requirements is an artificial rubber number that you inflate with a bicycle pump.

There is however one tree that comes to mind (or should I say, one of many?) which is close to the perfect tree for a small garden.

The plant in question is a variegated form of Chinese elm called, appropriately, *Ulmus parvifolia* 'Frosty'.

In its wild non-variegated form it comes from northern and central China, Korea, Taiwan and Japan and makes a lovely small spreading shade tree. Its leaves are small and dainty with a serrated edge and they sit neatly along the fan-shaped branches. When they shed they tend to fall down into the lawn, never to be seen again. If they are in such superabundance that the lawn can't swallow them, a quick run over with the mower will turn them into compost.

Once the tree matures its bark becomes a major asset. It tends to flake off in rounded pieces, exposing different shades of grey, brown and fawn.

It is hardy and quick-growing as well as tolerant of all the aforementioned conditions such as poor soil, drought, wind, wet feet and summer heat. The only drawback with *U. parvifolia* is that it doesn't usually satisfy clients when I tell them that the only other colour (apart from green leaves and nice bark) that they are likely to get is the copper colour that the tiny papery seeds produce as they ripen and prepare to shed. Before we move on, I feel I should point out that Chinese elms don't seem to be susceptible to Dutch elm disease nor do they have a particularly aggressive root system. They also endear themselves to me because they don't sucker, as many other elms do.

It is in the colour stakes that *U. parvifolia* 'Frosty' comes into its own. When its foliage first erupts in spring it is a soft yellow colour slightly marked with white. To me it is as pretty as any flowering blossom and has the advantage that no matter what the weather is like the display won't be ruined. By late spring the yellow is fading to mid green, leaving just the serrated edges of the leaves white. This gives the tree its characteristic frosty appearance throughout summer and autumn until the leaves again turn yellow before shedding. So you will have showy leaves throughout spring, summer and autumn and of course the attractive bark all year round once it is mature enough. Not too bad an effort for any hardy small deciduous tree, if you ask me.

U. parvifolia 'Frosty' is not as large-growing in height or width as the species. It can be expected to grow to about 7 metres tall by 3 metres wide (23 ft by 10 ft) in about ten

years. Its foliage will cast a soft dappled shade, dense enough to give a cool spot but not so thick that the lawn dies.

Why it isn't in every garden centre I really can't say. It is best grafted onto seedling Chinese elm but that can't be holding back sales, after all most of the roses and fruit trees (both edible and ornamental) that nurseries stock are budded or grafted.

I hope my writing about it may stimulate some interest in this sadly neglected plant, just so long as it doesn't become as common as muck.

Vestia foetida

A charming small evergreen shrub of elegant form that I have a passion for is an obscure member of the Solanaceae family, which means that it is related to such plants as tomatoes, potatoes, deadly nightshade, henbane and tobacco. A large number of this family, including the last three, are decidedly poisonous. The manufacturers of tobacco may wish to disagree.

Vestia is one of those monotypic genera, closely related to *Cestrum*.

Like so many other plants, our shrub has been known under more than one name. It was introduced some time before 1809 to the Berlin Botanic Garden, and when the botanist Willdenow set up the genus he named this species *Vestia lycioides*. However the plant had previously been called *Periphragmos foetidus* by Ruiz and Pavon in 1799. The genus *Periphragmos* has since disappeared, with most of its members now in the genus *Cantua*. The Vestia genus was not transferred. This doesn't mean that the epithet *foetidus* can be ignored, so the name of *Vestia foetida* should probably be the accepted one. It is also a fairly appropriate species name, as I will later explain.

It is a relatively easy and quick-growing evergreen shrub to about 2 metres (6 ft) tall with upright stems that arch slightly and attractively at the tips. A fully grown plant can be expected in as little as one or two years, so it is ideal for the impatient or if you need to fill a spot fast as your garden will be open to the public in a few months.

If it is planted in a well-drained but not dry spot in the sun or semi-shade all should be well. The only other thing I would suggest is a solid stake as it can have the unfortunate habit of falling over because its roots don't seem to be able to keep up with its top.

Like so many fast-growing shrubs it can be somewhat short-lived. If you decide that you can't live without it, it is as easy as a fuchsia to strike from cuttings. It will also tend to self-seed lightly for those who can't strike fuchsias. If you decide that you don't like it then it can go to God without you having to take matters into your own hands, leaving you with a nice gap for something else. I might add that I haven't got sick of it yet and find it a subtle and pleasing component of my blue and yellow border, surrounded by drifts of rich blue *Aquilegia alpina*.

The flowers consist of a narrow soft greenish-yellow trumpet about 3 cm ($1^1/4$ in) long with a tube-hugging green calyx. They are usually produced in respectable numbers from mid spring until mid or even late summer and are followed by yellow berries that stay around even longer.

Its leaves are a rich glossy green and they look good all year, but as one of its species names suggests they smell awful. I would suggest that you plant it back from the edge of the border so that you aren't assailed by the smell of burning rubber, except when you weed around it or prune it. You can of course have lots of fun with it and unsuspecting visitors.

I mentioned pruning a minute ago and if this is needed it should be done straight after flowering. Don't trim it as this will ruin its elegant habit. Instead, remove some of the older spent stems at the base. This will encourage new strong shoots from ground level and allow it to arch properly and show off its trumpets.

This shrub is often mistaken in my garden for an Australian correa, which may give you some idea of its ornamental value. It is of course not related and in fact comes from South America, from central Chile to be precise. It was introduced into England in

1815 and seems to have made little or no impact since, rarely getting more than a passing reference, usually about its stinky leaves.

The name honours Lorenz Chrysanth von Vest (1776-1840), an Austrian botanist and medico who was Professor of Medicine at Klagenfurt and then of Medicine, Botany and Chemistry at Graz. I can only wonder if he felt duly impressed having something smelly named after him. I know I wouldn't mind if someone felt I deserved to be honoured with a plant named after me, even if it was some weedy thing of no consequence. Taxonomists take note!

Viburnum opulus 'Notcutt's Variety'

What the very best form of any plant may be I guess is a personal choice, unless your nurseryman has described it himself and grows only one variety, leaving you no choice at all.

Flower power, even at the expense of other attributes like berries or good foliage, seems to be the direction many breeders and growers are going. Certainly the length of time that something is in bloom is important, however the size of the flowers and the extent to which they are produced on an average to well-grown plant should also be a consideration. Flower size is often obvious only when a plant is small and sitting in the nursery waiting for you to come along and buy it. It can be difficult to estimate the size of the flowers in proportion to the plant when it is fully grown. Generally speaking, smaller blooms on a large shrub will often make up for their lack of size with extra quantity and in many cases the end result is even better.

The other problem is that when buying something in bloom we often get carried away with the joys of the moment and don't even look to see if our chosen plant has attractive foliage, let alone ask if it does something in another season. For most of us, garden room is too precious for one week wonders.

All this is leading us somewhere and that is to *Viburnum opulus*, known as European Cranberry, although the real cranberry is *Vaccinium macrocarpon*, just to confuse the issue. The wild form of this viburnum is a large deciduous shrub to between 3 and 4 metres (10 to 13 ft), with attractive white lacecap-type flowers in spring. Lacecaps, for those who don't know, are heads of tiny flowers surrounded by sterile bracted blooms; they are often inexplicably (to me) called hen and chickens. I'll stick with lacecaps.

These are followed in summer by clusters of reddish berries and the leaves turn attractive shades in autumn. This succession of colour on a hardy shrub makes it a most valuable garden plant.

Some time about 1594 a sterile form with big balls of white bracted flowers was found. This is what we know as the guelder rose or snowball tree and it seems to have displaced the fertile fruiting forms in most nurseries. It certainly has showy flowers, but that is about it. This form, by the way, is called *V. opulus* 'Roseum', a far from appropriate but apparently more correct name than *V. opulus* 'Sterile', under which it is often offered. Much later (by several centuries) a new fertile form with larger lacecaps, wonderful clusters of translucent orange-red berries and extra good autumn foliage was discovered and named *V. opulus* 'Notcutt's Variety'. It probably came from or was named after the famous English nursery of that name.

It has never caught on like the guelder rose and yet when people see it in my garden I almost have to fight them off. It received an Award of Merit in 1930 and an Award of Garden Merit in 1984, so the English appreciate it.

In passing, I would like to mention *Viburnum opulus* 'Xanthocarpum', which is just as good but with yellow berries. This received an Award of Merit in 1932, a First Class Certificate in 1966 and an Award of Garden Merit in 1969.

Wigandia caracasana

In Victorian times gardening was probably one of the few universal pastimes. It was enjoyed by young and old, rich and poor, and was considered an entertainment as well as a productive hobby.

It must be stressed that the entertainment side was particularly important. Many were too isolated for regular theatre nights and unless Aunty Maude could play the piano or trombone you were probably left with reading or charades. I know that you could also go hunting if horses were your thing but my point really is that one had to find one's own fun before the invention of cinema, radio and television.

Victorians had a childlike fascination with practical jokes as well as anything odd or bizarre and it was in the garden that they could fully exploit these themes. A truly ugly or blood-thirsty statue might well get the desired effect. Stinking lilies were probably considered a great laugh and fasciated ferns or curly cactus were as popular as bearded ladies and two-headed sheep.

Enormous leaves were also highly regarded. These gave a tropical effect to the garden which allowed imaginations to run wild. One could pretend to be an African explorer searching for Dr Livingstone in the backyard or an intrepid botanist making his way up a South American river to find one of those giant waterlilies with leaves big enough to stand on.

It is something of a shame that in this day and age we tend to keep our entertainment indoors. We are led along by designers who tell us how our gardens should look and the current crop of experts who tell us what it is fashionable to plant. Most of us are too timid to just do what we want to and in the end we all get a terribly tasteful effect. The only fun we get is sneering at those lesser beings who inexplicably love cactus, garden gnomes or swans made out of rubber tyres.

This is all leading up to a dramatic foliage plant that was much loved by Victorian gardeners and in cold climates is still often raised as an annual for that period style of gardening, tropical bedding.

Wigandia caracasana is certainly no annual in more or less frost-free climates and can make a spreading small tree of 5 metres (16 ft 6 in) or so, more than big enough to swing through its branches.

The leaves are like big light green paddles and can measure 60 cm by 45 cm (2 ft by 18 in). To see a well-grown specimen is to be transported to the jungles of its native lands in Mexico, Colombia and Venezuela. Be sure to have an Aztec costume and a few virgins to sacrifice to the sun gods!

These leaves are rough-textured with scalloped edges and covered with fine lustrous slightly stinging hairs. Just think of the fun we can have introducing our unsuspecting visitors to the tactile aspects of the foliage. I might add that it isn't as dramatic as upending guests in the nettle patch nor is it as long-lasting in its effects.

Unlike so many other foliage plants, its floral attributes will be much admired. For a considerable time during the warmer months it will produce large panicles of rich mauve trumpet-shaped flowers with a white throat. These are about 2 cm ($^3/4$ in) long and will make a most impressive display.

Once you have one you needn't stop there as *Wigandia* is fairly easy to raise from seeds or suckers. If it hasn't produced any suckers, a quick spring through the bed with a sharp spade severing a few roots will start the ball rolling. Before you know it you will probably need a native guide to find the clothes line.

If its suckering tendencies daunt you, plant it as a lawn specimen then you can play Queen of Hearts with the lawnmower and 'off with their heads'.

Wigandia was named after Johannes Wigand (1523-1587), who was Bishop of Pomerania and a writer on Prussian plants. As there isn't any obvious connection between him and Mexico, one must assume he didn't collect it whilst converting the savages.

To grow it well, make sure that the aspect is sheltered from strong winds and frost. The soil should be kept moist in summer to encourage large leaves but well-drained in winter. I might add that I have a plant growing manfully at Macedon under a large eucalyptus to protect it from the frost. It will never grow vigorously in such a position or climate but it has survived several cold winters and I think it is also great fun to attempt unlikely plantings.

If you want to add a finishing touch to your planting of *Wigandia caracasana* why not install an Aztec altar or a ring of poison spears?

Zenobia pulverulenta

When someone asks for a lily-of-the-valley tree they are most likely to mean a *Clethra*, which produces lovely white scented flowers in late summer, although I think it is pushing the imagination to consider them much like those of the famous lily-of-the-valley (*Convallaria majalis*).

You may however have meant that you wanted a *Pieris*, which was once known as and is still sometimes called *Andromeda*. The flowers of this plant are produced in spring; they are non-scented and do look somewhat more like lily-of-the-valley. Most are however no more than shrubs, and even the biggest of them could only be called shrubs that have got above their station in life.

Another shrub with flowers like lily-of-the-valley which may help confuse the issue even further is *Zenobia pulverulenta*. I have never heard it called lily-of-the-valley anything but it looks as much like it as any of the above.

It is a member of the family Ericaceae, so you should immediately understand its requirements. For those that don't, they simply need a cool aspect and a compost-enriched acid soil. In other words, treat it as you would a rhododendron.

The Hillier Manual of Trees and Shrubs suggests that 'this glorious little shrub flowers during the "London Season", how else can it have been so unnoticed'. In Australia we don't even have this excuse, so hop to it.

It is a monotypic genus consisting of *Z. pulverulenta*, which is sometimes listed as *Z. speciosa* and comes from the eastern United States.

This elegant shrub rarely exceeds 1 metre (3 ft) tall and with its arching lax habit would be ideal to fill a small gap in a border of azaleas. As it flowers in early summer it will not have to compete with its more flamboyant bedfellows for attention. The pure white flowers are comparatively large, slightly scented and produced in clusters towards the tips of the branches. New growth is produced back along the stems behind the flowers, so you need to prune out the flowered wood. This can be done when it finishes flowering, although I like to pick sprays for the house so some pruning whilst in bloom has much to recommend it. The vase life of the flowers is quite extended and if it ever became available to the florist trade I'm sure it would be snapped up.

The foliage can be semi-evergreen or deciduous. This may be environmental, although I have a feeling that there may well be different forms in commerce. The leaves are entire with a wavy edge and about 6 cm (2^1/2 in) long, nothing much to get excited about but they are attached to pretty copper-coloured stems.

If you don't have a spot with appropriate soil you could try growing it in a tub of good potting mix. Being in a pot also means that it can be shifted around as needs be and that its lovely flowers will be lifted up closer to eye level for your convenience.

When siting it around the garden try and have it in front of something with deep green foliage as this will set off the flowers best.

Zenobia is easily propagated from layers or the suckers that it frequently produces, although commercially it is usually struck from summer cuttings under mist spray with a little bottom heat.

I am sure this elegant little shrub will please you and I'm sure the Queen of Palmyra after whom it was named would have been flattered. This naming was obviously done posthumously as she lived sometime around 266 AD and *Zenobia* was brought into cultivation in 1801. Since then, it has collected an Award of Merit in 1932 and a First Class Certificate in 1934.

Specialist Nurseries

AUSTRALIA

My nursery, Dicksonia Rare Plants, stocks all the trees and shrubs described in this book.

I have had satisfactory dealings with the other two nurseries, which I happily recommend.

Dicksonia Rare Plants, 686 Mount Macedon Road, Mount Macedon, Victoria 3441.
Tel: (03) 5426 3075
No mail order.

Woodbank Nursery, 2040 Huon Road, Longley, Tasmania 7150
Tel: (03) 6239 6452
Mail order

Yamina Rare Plants, 25 Moores Road, Monbulk, Victoria 3793
Tel: (03) 9756 6335
Mail order.

NEW ZEALAND

It is some years since I was in New Zealand, so I cannot speak from personal experience of the nurseries listed below. Their owners tell me that they stock many of the plants in this book, though they are not necessarily all available on a regular basis.

North Island

Cave's Tree Nursery, Pukeroro, RD 3, Hamilton. Tel/fax: (07) 827 6601

Dene's Garden Way, St Hill Lane, PO Box 8019, Havelock North.
Tel/fax: (06) 877 7162
Email: denes.gardenway@clear.net.nz

Top Trees Nursery Ltd, Ferry Road, Clive, Hawke Bay. Tel/fax: (06) 870 0082
Email: toptrees@inhb.co.nz

South Island

Blue Mountain Nurseries, 99 Bushy Hill Street, Tapanui. Tel: (03) 204 8250
Fax: (03) 204 8278

Trott's Garden & Nursery, Racecourse Road, No 6 RD, Ashburton. Tel: (03) 308 9530

Glossary

acid	Describes a soil in which the pH value is less than 7 in a scale ranging from 1 to 14.
alkaline	The opposite of acid. Used to describe a soil in which the pH value is more than 7. Alkaline soils are high in lime.
axil	The angle between the leaf and the stem that bears it.
bipinnate	Divided twice; used of leaves or fronds.
bract	Modified leaves at the base of a flower stalk or surrounding small individual flowers; sometimes coloured other than green and mistaken for the flower itself.
calyx	Outer covering of flower base, usually green, which protects buds; the individual sections of a calyx are called sepals.
clone	A plant derived by vegative reproduction, e.g. by a cutting, from one individual plant and therefore similar in all respects to the parent plant.
coppicing	Pruning to a stump or a collection of stumps at or just above ground level on a regular basis. *See* pages 28, 162.
corolla	Petals forming the inner ring of flower parts
cultivar	A plant that has been created by selective breeding, denoted by a distinctive name printed in inverted commas, e.g. *Cornus* 'Eddies White Wonder'. Unlike a variety, which occurs naturally in the wild.
dehiscense	The natural bursting open of fruits, etc. for the release of seeds or spores.
dioecious	Having male and female flowers on separate plants.
drupe	A fruit consisting of a thin outer skin, a succulent fleshy layer and a hard inner layer, enclosing (usually) a single seed, e. g. a plum.
espalier	Plant grown against a wall, usually having a single main stem and horizontally spread lateral branches.
family	A broad group of plants made up of genera thought to have derived from a common ancestral stock. Family names usually end in -aceae, e.g. Magnoliaceae, the Magnolia family.
fastigiate	Shaped like a pencil.
form	A sub-group within a species.
genus	A classification of plants below the level of a family and above the level of a species; plural, genera. A plant name usually consists of the genus name, written with a capital initial, and a species name, e.g. *Malus trilobata*, which is a member of the Rose family, Rosaceae.
glaucous	Covered with a bloom, giving a white, pale blue or greyish lustre.
humus	Well-decayed organic matter.
hybrid	The progeny of two different species in the same genus. *See also* ×.
inflorescence	A cluster of flowers.
monocarp	A plant that dies after having once borne fruit.
monotypic	Having only one species (used of a genus).
node	The point on a stem from which the leaf grows.
pH	A unit for measuring positive and negative ions in soil or other media; a measure of acidity or alkalinity in a scale ranging from 1 to 14. Too high or too low a pH will prevent nutrients from being absorbed.

panicle	A compound flower cluster in which the main stem carries racemes of stalked flowers, e.g. lilac.
pedicel	The stalk of an individual flower.
petiole	The stem that holds a leaf onto a branch and later sheds with the leaf.
pinnate	Divided once; used of leaves or fronds.
pollarding	Method of pruning a tree in which all growth at or below the desired height is pruned back to the same stub. *See* pages 28, 162.
raceme	An arrangement of flowers on short stalks, usually of nearly equal length, arising from an elongated stem , e.g. foxglove, lily-of-the-valley.
section	In botanical classification a group of plants with common characteristics, coming between a genus and its species. A section may consist of one or several species.
sepal	Leaf-like segments that together make up the calyx of a flower. They are usually green and inconspicuous, but may be colourful.
sessile	Of a part of a plant borne without a support, e.g. a leaf without a petiole.
species	A classification of closely related plants within a genus. Abbreviated to sp., plural spp.
stamen	The male reproductive part of a flower.
stigma	The tip of a style, carrying pollen-receptive tissue.
stipule	One of a pair of leaf-like growths (sometimes thorns) at the base of a petiole.
style	A narrow extension of the ovary, bearing the stigma at its apex.
tomentose	Furry.
trifoliate	Divided into three leaflets
variety	A plant belonging to a species but differing slightly from the type specimen from which the botanical description of the species was originally prepared. Unlike a cultivar, a variety occurs naturally in the wild.
×	Symbol used to indicate a hybrid, e.g. *Salix* × *boydii*. Usually used only when the hybrid has been given a Latin name, to distinguish it from a species. This practice is no longer allowed and hybrids must now be given a non-Latin name, e.g. *Hypericum* 'Rowallane'.

Bibliography

GENERAL

I have used the following books most frequently in the course of writing my plant profiles:

Bean, William Jackson. *Trees and Shrubs Hardy in the British Isles*. 8th ed. London, Murray, 1970-1988. 4 v. plus Supplement.

Harrison, Richmond E. *Handbook of Trees and Shrubs*. 5th ed. rev. Wellington, Reed, 1974.

The Hillier Manual of Trees and Shrubs. 6th ed. Newton Abbot (Devon), David & Charles, 1991.

Krüssmann, Gerd. *Manual of Cultivated Broad-leaved Trees and Shrubs*. Beaverton (Oregon), Timber Press, 1984. 3 v.

Royal Horticultural Society. *The New Royal Horticultural Society Dictionary of Gardening*; editor-in-chief Anthony Huxley. London, Macmillan, 1992. 4 v.

PLANT NAMES

Stearn, William T. *Dictionary of Plant Names for Gardeners: a Handbook on the Origin and Meaning of the Botanical Names of some Cultivated Plants*. Rev. enl. ed. London, Cassell, 1992.

HISTORY OF PLANT COLLECTING

W.J. Bean, Hillier and the RHS *Dictionary* all have sections on plant collecting and individual collectors. For those seeking more detail, the following titles are suggested:

Coats, Alice M. *The Quest for Plants . . . Horticultural Pioneers . . . from the Renaissance to the Twentieth Century*. London, Studio Vista, 1969. [Also pub. as *The Plant Hunters*. New York, McGraw Hill, 1970]

Musgrave, Toby, and others. *The Plant Hunters: Two Hundred Years of Adventure and Discovery around the World*. London, Ward Lock, 1998

Whittle, Michael Tyler. The Plant Hunters. London, Heinemann, 1970 [Also The Lyons Press & *Horticulture Magazine*, New York, 1997, in Horticulture Garden Classics series]

Index of Plant Names

This index includes:
Common names of profiled trees and shrubs
Botanical and/or common names of plants suitable as companions for profiled trees and shrubs
Botanical and/or common names of selected additional plants
For botanical names of profiled trees and shrubs, *see* the Table of Contents.